New

dollar store décor

dollar store décor

décor

101 Projects for Lush Living that Won't Break the Bank

MARK MONTANO

universe

First published in the United States
of America in 2005 by
UNIVERSE PUBLISHING
A Division of Rizzoli International
Publications, Inc.
300 Park Avenue South
New York, NY 10010
www.rizzoliusa.com

2004 2005 2006 2007/ 10 9 8 7 6 5 4 3 2 1

Printed in the United States of America

Design by Paul Kepple and Susan Van Horn @
Headcase Design
www.headcasedesign.com

Photos by Jeremy Nelson

ISBN: 0-7893-1303-0

Library of Congress Catalog Control Number:
2005900329

Note: This book is intended to be fun and
informative. However, care should be exercised to ensure that the materials used are
nontoxic, that candles and lamps are not left
unattended, that proper ventilation is pro-
vided, and that caution is exercised in handling
sharp tools or objects.

This book is dedicated to my mom for always showing me that possibilities can exist in places where you would least expect to find them.

contents

special thanks

Jorge Montano

Thelma Linton

Michael Carolan

David Hart

Jeremy Nelson

Josie Shotwell

Arielle Eckstut

Kathleen Jayes

Phillip Montano

The cast of *While You Were Out*

introduction

When I was growing up as one of six boys, we really had to stretch a dollar!

I remember going to Six Star, the local dollar store, with my mom and thinking, "Get me out of this junk store!" And then something magical happened. My mother's creative eye transformed the trashy objects surrounding us into treasures: Suddenly, candles, bags of beads, and marbles became raw materials of creative expression. We made the most amazing discoveries together: frames that could be painted, rugs that could be turned into pillows, beads that could be made into curtains, whisks that could become wind chimes, and all the glitter, glue, and paint to make it happen. Recently I was buying cleaning supplies in a dollar store in New York City and found myself reminded of those times. I became inspired to make this book.

I know what you are thinking: What can I possibly find at the dollar store that would look great in my home? Well, the answer is just about anything! All you need is a little creativity. Plus, the price is right and you have an endless amount of objects from all over the world in one place. Why should you spend $25 on a wall clock when you can transform a dollar store wall clock into a work of art? Why should you spend $100 on a gift for someone when making them something fantastic and personal, such as a lace tablecloth for their new home or place mats for their first dinner party, would mean so much more? I hope this book helps you realize that more expensive doesn't always mean better and that just because something costs 99 cents doesn't mean it's cheap—just well priced!

Good luck with all the projects you make and don't forget to enjoy yourself! If you have a question or just want to keep in touch with me, I am always here at the other end of your computer at markmontanonyc@aol.com.

Love,
Mark!

① rag rug pillow

YOU NEED:

- 1 rag rug,
- pillow stuffing,
- sewing machine,
- thread

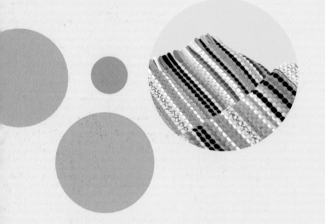

This project is really easy! I like rag rugs because they are colorful, sturdy, and they match any décor. They come in a wonderful array of colors and look handmade. Just make sure you pick one that looks the same on both sides.

1) Fold your rug in half and stitch around the edges using a ½-inch seam allowance, leaving a 5-inch hole for stuffing. You might also want to use a heavy-duty needle on your machine, since this type of rug can be quite thick.

2) Turn the pillow inside out so that the seams are now on the inside.

3) Fill the pillow with the stuffing and hand stitch the hole with a needle and thread.

$$: To save money, use a bed pillow for stuffing. You can stuff two rag rug pillows with the contents of one bed pillow at a cost of $3 to $5, which is often less expensive than buying a bag of stuffing.

2 party bag mirror

YOU NEED:

- colorful party bag,
- color photocopies of the bag on sticker paper,
- mirror with flat frame,
- McCloskey water-based polyurethane,
- small brush,
- scissors

For this frame I took an element from a party bag that I thought would look great when repeated on a mirror frame. It is easiest to apply your stickers to a mirror with a flat frame.

1) Cut out any of the patterns you like from a party bag. Paste them onto an 8½" x 11" piece of paper.

2) Take this paper to a copy shop and have them make color copies on sticker paper. The number of copies you need will depend on the amount of pattern you can fit on the page and the size of your mirror.

3) Cut out your designs from the sticker paper, peel away the backing, and apply the stickers to the edge of your mirror.

4) After you have applied your design, carefully apply the water-based polyurethane to the design with a small brush. If you get polyurethane on the mirror, wipe it off with a damb cotton swab while it's still wet, making sure not to wet the sticker paper with your swab.

5) Once the polyurethane dries, you will be able to clean your mirror with glass cleaner.

③ color pencil frame

YOU NEED:
- **color pencils,**
- **frame,**
- **Elmer's wood glue,**
- **small saw (optional),**
- **pencil sharpener,**
- **sandpaper**

Sometimes you can find color pencils that are about 3 inches long. If you can't, cut longer pencils in half.

1) Measure out your frame to see how many pencils you will need.
2) Sharpen the ends of the pencils so their different colors of lead are visible.
3) Gently sand your frame and one side of each pencil. Spread the glue around your frame and apply the pencils one by one, sanded side down, to the frame. Alternate light and dark colors and flip them around so that the tips point in different directions. Let dry overnight.

Bonus: This frame looks great filled with colorful art. I painted the picture here with a small brush using every watercolor in the box!

④ marble candleholder

YOU NEED:

- **a bag of marbles,**
- **drinking glasses in various sizes,**
- **epoxy glue,**
- **candles**

Don't lose your marbles over this project! It's really easy and can turn any simple drinking glass into a great candleholder! The marbles catch the light of the flame, and using glasses of different heights together looks fantastic.

1) Select your glasses. It's best to use glasses that have a groove on the bottom in which to set your marbles so they don't roll off while you are gluing them.

2) Set your glass upside down on a piece of newspaper. Always be sure to have proper ventilation when using epoxy glues. Mix your epoxy on a paper plate. Apply the glue to the bottom of the glass with a toothpick and set your marbles in the glue.

3) Don't move your glass until the glue is set. Most epoxy glues take about 5 minutes to set, but read the instructions to be sure. The great thing about using epoxy is that it dries completely clear and is very strong.

⑤ party bag lamp shade

YOU NEED:

- large party bag,
- lamp shade,
- matching ribbon,
- hot glue gun and glue sticks,
- scissors,
- pencil

For this project you will need a large party bag. Buy the biggest one you can find! The one I used was about 18" x 24" inches.

1) Carefully cut your bag open so you end up with one large flat sheet of printed party bag paper.

2) Lay the bag printed side down on a flat surface. Your lamp shade should have a seam along its side. Place the shade on this seam near one edge of the bag. Starting at the seam, roll your shade on the paper, tracing a line along the top of the shade with your pencil as it rolls, until you get to the seam again. Line up the shade at the starting point again, and this time, trace a line along the bottom of the shade. You should end up with two parallel lines on the paper. Connect the ends of these lines with straight edges and cut out the shape. This pattern should fit around your shade perfectly.

3) With a hot glue gun, tack the paper around the shade at the top and bottom. Trim off any excess.

4) Hot-glue your ribbon onto the seam of the shade to cover it and then around the top and the bottom of the shade.

Now light up your life!

⑥ domino frame

YOU NEED:

- frame,
- dominoes,
- hot glue gun and glue sticks,
- pencil,
- sandpaper

1) Sand the frame and the backs of the dominoes. Sanding will help the dominoes stick to the glue.

2) Lay your dominoes on your frame to determine how many you will need for this project. I used 34 small dominoes on a 5" x 7" frame. Mark their placement with a pencil.

3) Apply a 2" line of glue to the frame, and add your dominoes. Glue only one or two dominoes at a time because hot glue dries quickly.

Take your time and you will end up with a winner!

7 decorative domino tray

YOU NEED:

- **dominoes,**
- **hot glue gun and glue sticks,**
- **epoxy glue,**
- **two handles,**
- **8" x 10" frame with a flat edge,**
- **sandpaper**

This is one of my favorite projects because it's so beautiful that everyone asks me where I bought it!

1) Remove the glass and the stand from the back of your frame so it lies flat like a tray.

2) Sand the frame and the backs of the dominoes.

3) Place your dominoes on and around the frame to make sure you will have enough to cover the edges and the center. I used 82 large dominoes to cover an 8" x 10" frame. Mark their placement with a pencil.

4) Starting with the center of the tray, hot glue one or two dominoes at a time because hot glue dries quickly.

5) After you have applied enough dominoes to cover the center, apply them around the edges. Use a lot of glue and let it set for several minutes.

6) Carefully sand your handles and the edges of the frame where you will be applying them. Making sure you have proper ventilation, mix your epoxy glue on a paper plate and glue on the handles. Most epoxy glues take about 5 minutes to set. The great thing about using epoxy is that it dries completely clear and is very strong.

Caution: This tray is more decorative than useful, so be careful about putting too much weight on it.

⑧ party bag tray

YOU NEED:

- **one plastic tray,**
- **McCloskey Heirloom Crystal Clear Polyurethane,**
- **party bag,**
- **color photocopies of party bag**
- **pattern on sticker paper,**
- **pencil,**
- **paintbrush**

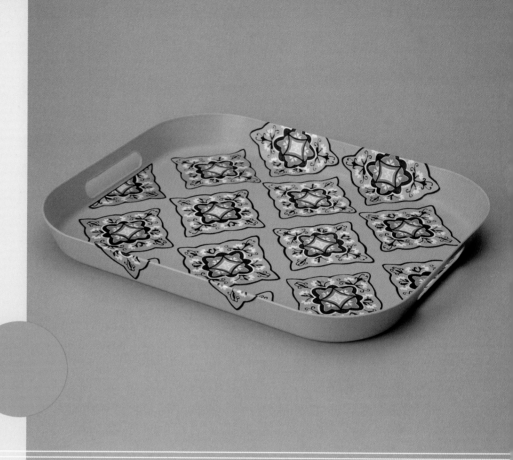

For this tray, I took an element of a party bag that I thought would make a neat design when repeated on a tray.

1) Cut out any of the patterns you like from a party bag. Paste them on an 8½" x 11" piece of paper.

2) Take this paper to a copy shop and have them make color copies on sticker paper. The number of copies you need will depend on the amount of pattern you can fit on the page and the size of your tray. I was able to get 6 squares on a piece of sticker paper and I needed 3 copies for this tray.

3) Cut out your designs, and play with their arrangement on the tray. When you're happy with how it looks, lightly pencil in their place-ment. Then peel off the stickers' backings, and apply them to your tray.

4) Using a small brush, carefully apply the water-based polyurethane to the tray. Once it's dry, you will be able to wipe your tray clean with a damp cloth.

9 clothespin frame

YOU NEED:

- **50 clothespins,**
- **8½" x 11" flat wood frame,**
- **Elmer's wood glue,**
- **sandpaper,**
- **pencil**

1) Remove the metal spring from each pin to create two pieces. Simply pull the ends apart and the spring will bend enough to fall off the pin and leave you with two pieces. I started with 50 clothespins for this project; after removing the pins, I had 100 pieces to glue around the frame.

2) Sand the frame and the back of each clothespin. Sanding helps the glue stick, which will make your frame nice and sturdy.

3) Place your clothespins around the frame to determine how many you will need. Mark their placement with a pencil and then glue the pins around the frame. It takes a while for Elmer's wood glue to dry so I recommend that you let it dry overnight.

Bonus: I made the art in this frame by folding a piece of yellow construction paper in half and cutting shapes along the fold. These designs have an primitive look and are easy to make. Give it a try!

10 domino coasters

YOU NEED:

- **dominoes,**
- **Plumber's Goop Glue,**
- **sturdy pieces of plastic that you can cut apart (like a heavy-duty plastic folder from the school supply section in the dollar store),**
- **sandpaper,**
- **pencil,**
- **scissors**

These coasters will look fabulous at your next party, and they make a super hostess gift!

1) Arrange 8 dominoes in a square on top of the plastic and with a pencil trace around them (the coasters pictured here are 4" x 4"). Try to get the dominoes near the edge of the plastic so you can get as many squares out of one piece as possible.

2) Cut out the squares from the plastic and scratch them with sandpaper. Then sand the backs of the dominoes.

3) Spread the glue on the plastic and apply the dominoes. Let it dry for about an hour.

Coast into the cocktail hour!

11 glass chip votive holder

YOU NEED:

- epoxy glue,
- cellophane tape,
- glass chips,
- drinking glass with smooth surface

Tip: I tried many glues for this project and the epoxy works the best. It takes some time, but it's worth it!

1) Find an octagonal glass with flat sides so your glass chips won't slide off while you're working.

2) Working in a well-ventilated area, mix your epoxy glue on a paper plate and use a toothpick to apply it to the glass. You can also dip your glass chip into the glue, but be careful not to get the glue on your fingers. Carefully place your glass chips onto one edge of the glass and let them set for about 5 minutes. Once that side has set, rotate the glass and do another line of glass chips. Repeat, doing one line of chips at a time, until the whole glass is covered.

Insert a candle and watch it sparkle!

12 woven multicolor rug place mat

YOU NEED:

- sewing machine,
- rag rugs,
- matching thread,
- washable matching ribbon,
- scissors

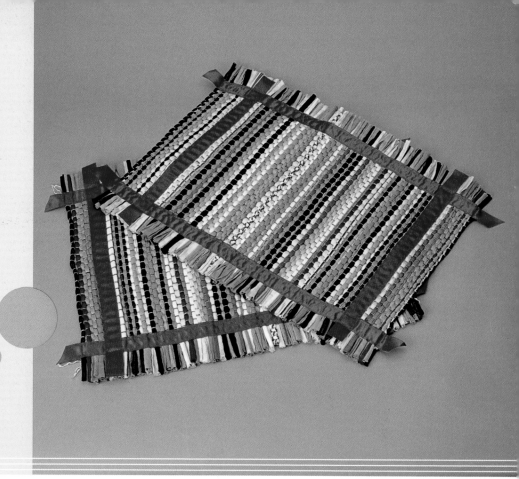

One rug will make 2 place mats.

1) Cut the rug in half. Unravel about 1 inch of the cut edge so it matches the fringed side of the rug.

2) Cut your ribbon into 4 pieces, making each piece about 2 inches longer than the fringed side of the mat it will trim. I used a 1-inch-wide, washable poly-satin ribbon.

3) Pin the ribbons to the fringed edges of both place mats and stitch around each side of the ribbon with a zigzag stitch.

4) Trim the ends of the ribbons at an angle.

Set the table!

13 snug as a bug in a rug bag

YOU NEED:

- ¼ yard of vinyl,
- pinking sheers,
- 18" x 24" rag rug,
- sewing machine,
- matching thread

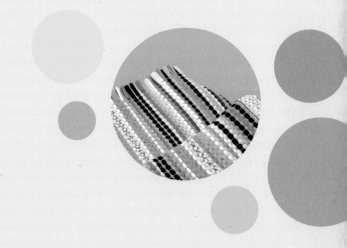

This project requires more skill, but I think you can do it!

1) From the vinyl, cut 2 pieces that are each as long as the width of the rug and 4" wide. (Set aside the leftover vinyl to make handles.) Scallop one side of each piece.

2) Sew both scalloped pieces onto opposite ends of the same side of the rug.

3) From the reserved vinyl, cut two 14" x 1" strips. Fold each in half lengthwise to make the handles. Stitch them closed using a ½-inch seam allowance. Leave one inch on each end of the handles unstitched.

4) Spread out the unstitched ends of the handles and sew them about 5 inches apart in the center of the scalloped vinyl trim. Stitch them several times.

5) Now take the rag rug and fold it in half with the handles and the trim on the inside. Sew the edges of the bag together leaving a ½-inch seam allowance, making sure to catch the vinyl at the sides.

6) To box out the corners, pinch the corners of the bag about 3 inches in from the bottom point. Stitch a line perpendicular to the side seam 3 inches up from the point. You can pin it first to see how it looks. Turn it inside out and you have your squared edge.

paint chip art

YOU NEED:

- **paint chips from the paint store,**
- **glue stick,**
- **frame,**
- **gold spray paint,**
- **newspaper,**
- **scissors,**
- **paper**

You can use white paper of any size for this project. I used an 8½" x 11" piece of card-stock paper.

1) Take several different strips of paint chips in one color scheme and cut them into 1" x 1" squares.

2) Spread out some newspaper in a well-ventilated area. Spray paint a regular piece of paper with gold spray paint, let it dry, and then cut it into ½" x ½" squares.

3) Using a glue stick, paste the paint chip squares onto a piece of white paper, leaving about ½" between each square. Glue the smaller gold squares on top of some of the paint chip squares. Keep going until you like it.

4) When it's finished, place it in a simple frame.

Instant art!

15 name frame napkin rings

YOU NEED:

- small frames,
- spray paint,
- newspaper,
- 8-inch long cable ties,
- Plumber's Goop Glue,
- sandpaper,
- paper for name tags

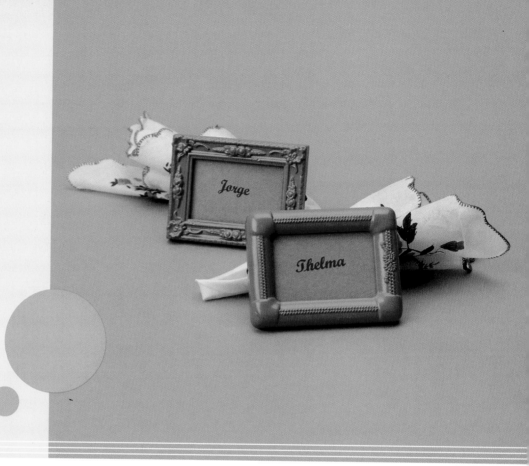

These are great for a dinner party or wedding! I bought four frames for 99 cents.

1) Remove the glass from each frame and set aside. Lay down newspaper in a well-ventilated area and spray paint the frames. (I used Leafy Green Krylon spray paint.) Let dry.

2) While they are drying, make loops with the cable ties.

3) Sand the back of each dry frame and spread on a generous amount of Plumber's Goop Glue. Gently place the cable loop in the glue on the back of the frame and let it dry. The loop should be sticking up so that when the glue dries you can insert your napkin.

4) After everything dries, assemble the frame, fill with the names of your guests (I printed mine from my computer onto pink construction paper), and pull your napkins through the rings! You can reuse these frames for other dinner parties—just change the names.

Tip: It would be nice to handwrite the names of your guests or, even better, include their photographs. Maybe you have one from a party or even one from your high school yearbook!

Dingdong, the guests have arrived and they have something fun to talk about when they see the amazing table you have set!

16 chop chop chopstick frames

YOU NEED:

- 20 chopsticks,
- the glass from a 5" x 7" or 4" x 6" frame,
- Elmer's wood glue,
- 1 foot of ribbon,
- pencil,
- sandpaper,
- newspaper

1) Sand one side of each chopstick.

2) Place the glass on a piece of newspaper. To figure out how you want to arrange your frame, place 5 chopsticks on one side of the glass, and 5 more on the opposite side of the glass. Layer the remaining 10 chopsticks (5 per side) on top of and perpendicular to the first two sides to complete the frame. Make sure that the chopsticks cover the edges of the glass.

3) Mark on the glass with a pencil where your first layer of chopsticks will be glued. Take them all away and spread the glue over your marked area. Then apply one set of chopsticks, sanded side down, to each side. When the glue's dry (it should take about a half hour), spread glue on the sanded side of the second set of chopsticks and layer these on top of and perpendicular to the first two sides to complete the frame. Let dry.

4. Turn the frame over to what is now the back and add a bead of glue all the way around where the chopsticks meet the glass. Let dry. This will make the frame stronger.

5) Glue the ends of the ribbon onto the back to create something from which to hang the frame. Skip this step if you want to lean the frame against a mirror, a shelf, or a wall. Tape your art on the back and enjoy!

17 chopstick candleholder

YOU NEED:

- **100 chopsticks,**
- **paper,**
- **pencil,**
- **Elmer's wood glue,**
- **tall candle in glass container**

Did you ever pile up popsicle sticks to make a box? Well, this is the same concept, but I used chopsticks instead! If you don't eat as much Chinese food as I do, just head to the dollar store and pick up a few packages of them for this project.

1) Place your candle on a piece of paper. Draw a square around the candle's base leaving about ½ inch on all sides. The square will serve as a guide while you build your holder.

2) Lay 2 chopsticks on opposite sides of the square. Dot their tops with glue where the second set of chopsticks for the other sides of the square will be placed. Keep building around the square, two sides at a time, until you have gone as high as your glass candle. Be careful not to use too much glue because it can drip down the sides and look just awful!

3) Let dry for a few hours.

18 chopstick trivet

YOU NEED:

- **24 chopsticks,**
- **Elmer's wood glue**

1) Place 12 chopsticks down parallel to one another, ¾ of an inch apart.

2) Dot the Elmer's wood glue every ½ inch along each chopstick. Lay the top set of 12 chopsticks across the first, making a perfect grid. Be careful not to use too much glue because it can drip down the sides and look just awful.

3) Let dry for a few hours.

Use your trivet to hold a candle or a hot dish.

table garden
place mats

YOU NEED:
- **simple place mats in solid colors,**
- **faux flowers,**
- **faux leaves,**
- **buttons,**
- **sewing machine,**
- **matching thread**

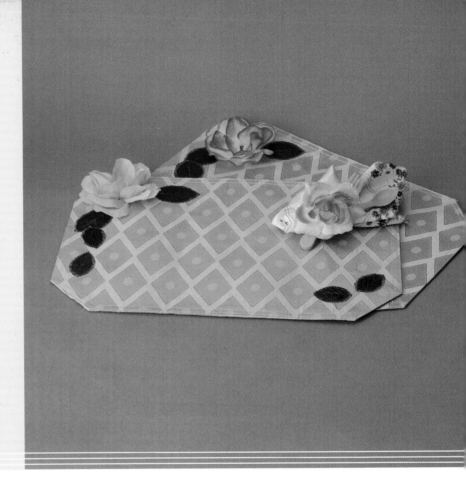

OK, maybe the pretty pink place mats at the dollar store are decorative enough, but as I always say, if you can make it even better, why not? With a few faux flowers and a button or two, your plain place mats will become a table garden.

1) Remove the stem from the plastic center of the faux flower and attach the flower with a straight pin to the upper-left-hand corner of the place mat.

2) Cut the leaves off the stem and pin them artfully onto the place mat below the flower and on the lower-right-hand corner.

3) Using the button stitch on your sewing machine or a needle and thread, attach a button in the center of the flower while at the same time attaching it to the place mat.

4) With your sewing machine set on zigzag stitch, sew all the way around each leaf to keep them in place.

5) Clip your threads and set a wonderful table.

Tip: These place mats look great with the napkin rings on page 46.

kitchen utensil clock

YOU NEED:

- **clock,**
- **Plumber's Goop Glue,**
- **plastic spoons**

What is more perfect than a kitchen clock decorated with utensils? I used baby spoons because I like the colors.

1) Sand all the way around the edge of your clock. Then sand the back of the end of every spoon and fork that you will be gluing to the clock. We used 32 utensils in all, but make sure you get an idea of how many you will need to complete the project before you start gluing.

2) Working on a flat surface, spread the Goop glue around the edge of the clock and attach your utensils. Goop glue doesn't dry quickly, so you can be generous with it and cover the entire clock before adding the utensils.

3) Do not move the clock for at least 2 hours.

Tell time tastefully!

21 flowery fruit bowl

YOU NEED:

- **McCloskey Heirloom Crystal Clear Polyurethane,**
- **small paintbrush,**
- **flowered party bag,**
- **color photocopies of the bag on sticker paper,**
- **scissors,**
- **Elmer's glue,**
- **bowl with smooth surface,**
- **pencil,**
- **8½ x 11 piece of paper**

For this fruit bowl, I took an element of a party bag that I thought would make a neat design when repeated.

1) Cut out any flowers you like from a party bag. Paste them on an 8½" x 11" piece of paper.

2) Take this paper to a copy shop and have them make color copies on sticker paper. The number of copies you need will depend on the amount of pattern you can fit on the page and the size of your bowl.

I was able to get 5 clusters of flowers onto a piece of sticker paper and I needed 15 clusters for this bowl, so that meant 3 copies.

3) Cut out your designs, and play with their arrangement on the bowl. When you're happy with how it looks, lightly pencil in their placement. Then peel off the stickers' backings, and apply them to your bowl.

4) With a small brush, carefully paint the water-based polyurethane over the bowl. Once it's dry, you will be able to wipe it clean with a damp cloth.

This bowl looks great displayed on a table or a shelf.

Caution: This bowl is primarily decorative and great for dry items such as fresh fruit or chips, but stay away from wet things like spaghetti!

22 rose bouquet lamp shade

YOU NEED:

- **25 to 30 faux flowers and leaves,**
- **small lamp shade,**
- **hot glue gun and glue sticks,**
- **scissors**

I have been making these lamp shades forever and now I see them being sold everywhere for a lot of money! You can illuminate your life by making this one in a half hour for just a few dollars.

1) Select a bunch of faux flowers that match your décor. I used fuzzy red roses because they looked rich when bundled together. The number of flowers you need will depend on the size of your shade. Don't worry about buying too many flowers, because you can always use them for the other flower projects in the book!

2) Remove the flowers and leaves from the stems. With a hot glue gun, start applying the roses all around the shade in rows. Random patterns look good, too.

3) When you have completed the flowers, dot in leaves as accents wherever you see a blank spot. I like to make the leaves stick out a bit to give more dimension to the shade.

23 bed of roses flower pillow

YOU NEED:

- **two 21" x 21" inch squares of heavy pink fabric,**
- **pillow stuffing,**
- **25 buttons,**
- **12 red and 12 pink faux flowers,**
- **cellophane tape,**
- **a sewing machine or a needle and thread**

I made this pillow 20" by 20", but you can make yours any size you want.

1) Take apart the flowers and remove all of the plastic parts and stems from them. They should come off easily with a little tug.

2) Pin the flowers in position on one of the squares, leaving a border of about 2 inches all the way around the pillow. This way, when you are sewing the pillow squares together, you won't get the petals caught in the seams. After you have pinned your flowers in position, zigzag or hand-stitch a button on the center of each one. I alternated colors, and with some of the flowers I mixed the pink and red petals together.

3) After all the flowers are attached with buttons, fold the flowers on the edge toward the center and tape them down. This will help keep them out of the seam when you attach the back of the pillow.

4) Place the other pink square on top of the flowers (make sure the side you want showing is facing on the flowers) and stitch the 2 squares together, leaving a 5-inch hole.

5) Turn the pillow right side out, remove the tape, and fill it with pillow stuffing. Stitch your 5-inch hole closed with a needle and thread.

Spray with your favorite perfume and have sweet dreams!

24 table garden napkin rings

YOU NEED:

- faux flowers,
- 8-inch-long cable ties,
- needle and thread,
- buttons,
- hot glue gun and glue sticks

This is a quick way to make any table look fresh and springy.

1) Take apart your faux flowers, being sure to remove any plastic pieces. The plastic can make it difficult to push your needle through the flower when you are sewing.

2) Pin the flower petals together in an arrangement you like.

3) Make a loop with your cable tie that is big enough for a napkin to slip through. With your needle and thread, stitch a button into the center of your flower and sew it to the cable tie. Do this several times to secure the flower to the cable tie.

4) Add a dot of hot glue onto the thread to make it even more secure. You might also want to add a dot of hot glue inside the mouth of the cable tie so it doesn't get any smaller.

Add your napkin and bon appétit!

25 pop art portrait

YOU NEED:

- photo,
- **enlarged copies of the photo**
- cellophane tape,
- **colored cellophane plastic,**
- **Lucite box frame,**
- scissors

This takes some experimenting, but the result is worth it.

1) Enlarge your photo on the light setting of a photocopier to twice its size. It should be about 8½" by 11".

2) Cut that picture into 4 equal pieces and enlarge each one of them to twice their size. This should make your picture about 17" x 22". If you want to make it even bigger, cut these pieces into 4 equal pieces and repeat.

3) Carefully cut off the white edges, making sure not to cut into the photo at all. Tape the pictures together to create one very large photo. Because you are enlarging the photo on a lighter setting, the features should start to become more graphic.

4) This is where the experimenting comes in. Now that you have your large black-and-white photo, you need to find a frame that is big enough for it.

5) I used a clear plastic box frame that cost about $11. Tape the photo to the frame and then tape a layer of colored cellophane—you know, the clear stuff they use for gift wrapping—over it. It will color your photograph, giving it a whole new look.

Tip: If you want to make an orange Warhol, you can use red and yellow cellophane together.

See you in the art gallery!

nothing-to-sneeze-at curtains and valance

YOU NEED:

- **20 printed handkerchiefs,**
- **sewing machine,**
- **matching thread,**
- **2 tension rods or curtain rods,**
- **pins,**
- **iron**

If you like a delicate, feminine look for your room, these are the perfect curtains for you. They are light and airy, and the flowers give any room a fresh, pretty feel.

1) Iron your handkerchiefs completely flat so they are easy to sew. Pin your handkerchiefs together, using 8 handkerchiefs per panel. Make 2 panels.

2) After you pin the handkerchiefs, carefully stitch them together using your sewing machine. The great thing about these curtains is that you don't have to hem them because the handkerchief is already finished with a beautiful scalloped edge.

3) To make a pocket for the curtain rod, fold the top edge of the panel over 1½ inches and stitch along the edge.

4) To make the valance, stitch four handkerchiefs together in a line. Fold over the top 1½ inches and stitch along the edge to make a pocket for the rod.

You can make the curtains and the valance longer by adding more handkerchiefs.

27 handkerchief tablecloth

YOU NEED:
- **16 printed handkerchiefs,**
- **sewing machine,**
- **matching thread,**
- **iron,**
- **pins**

This requires some sewing so whip out that sewing machine!

1) Thread your machine with some white thread and a white bobbin.
2) Iron your handkerchiefs completely flat so they are easy to sew. Pin them together in 4 rows of 4 handkerchiefs each. Stitch each row of 4 together with a straight stitch.
3) Clip the loose threads to keep your project neat before you move on to the next step.

5) Pin your rows of 4 side by side and stitch them together.
6) Clip your threads, iron again, and spread your new tablecloth.
$$: For about $10, you can make curtains and a matching tablecloth that will spruce up any kitchen!

grandma's lace doily curtains

YOU NEED:

- **12 rectangular or square lace doilies,**
- **sewing machine,**
- **pins,**
- **matching thread,**
- **curtain rod**

If you like an antique, turn-of-the-century feel, these lace doily curtains are perfect for you. They look hand-crocheted, and they let in a lot of light.

1) Pin your doilies together 6 per panel and make 2 panels.

2) Carefully stitch the doilies together on your sewing machine. One of the great things about these curtains is that you don't have to hem them, because the doily is already finished with a beautiful crocheted edge.

3) To make your curtain rod pocket in the top of the panel, just fold the top edge over 1½ inches and stitch along the edge. If you don't want to sew a rod sleeve, you can carefully weave the curtain rod through the natural openings in the weave of the doilies.

You can make the curtains any size you want by adding more lace doilies.

29 grandma's lace doily tablecloth

YOU NEED:

- 9 to 12 rectangular or square lace doilies (depending on the size of table you are trying to cover),
- sewing machine,
- iron and spray starch,
- ivory thread,
- pins

This tablecloth is elegant and gives a wonderful antique feel to any table. It's not just for the kitchen—you can use it anywhere in the house, maybe over the back of an antique sofa.

1) Iron your doilies completely flat using starch so that they are easy to sew.

2) Pin them together in 3 separate rows of 4 doilies each, and then stitch each row of 4 together with a straight stitch. Clip the loose threads.

3) Pin your 3 rows of 4 side by side and stitch them together.

4) Clip the threads, iron again, and spread out your new tablecloth.

Together with the matching curtains, this tablecloth will turn an otherwise cold living room or kitchen into a place that Grandma would love to sit and have tea with you!

30 stripe-it-rich bathroom towel set

YOU NEED:

- **6 hand towels,**
- **sewing machine,**
- **matching thread,**
- **scissors**

I found striped towels in three different colors that looked wonderful together. With a few nips and tucks, I made a fantastic bathroom set!

1) To make your cozy bath towel, lay 3 hand towels side by side and stitch them together.

2) To make your lovely little washcloths, cut one hand towel in half and hem both pieces with your sewing machine.

3) Use the remaining 2 hand towels—already the perfect size—to complete the set.

My bathroom is every bright color under the sun, so the mix of stripes worked well. Plus, mixing colors is the best way to create an exciting look that no one else will have. You can also find hand towels in different patterns—look around and see what works with your décor. Everyone will wonder where you got this super cool bathroom towel set!

31 crisscross color pencil frame

YOU NEED:

- **20 color pencils,**
- **the glass from a 5" x 7" frame,**
- **Plumber's Goop Glue**

1) Sand one side of each pencil.

2) To figure out how you want to arrange your pencils, place 5 pencils on one side of the glass and 5 more on the opposite side of the glass. Layer the remaining 10 pencils (5 per side) on top of and perpendicular to the first two sides to complete the frame. Make sure that the pencils cover all the edges of the glass.

3) Mark on the glass where your first layer of pencils will be glued. Remove them and spread the glue over your marked area. Then apply the first set of pencils to each side, sanded side down. When the glue's dry (it should take about a half hour), spread glue on the sanded side of the second set of pencils and layer them on top of and perpendicular to the first two sides to complete the frame. Let dry.

4) Turn the frame over to what is now the back and add a bead of glue all the way around where the pencils meet the glass. Let dry. This will make the frame stronger.

5) Glue the ends of the ribbon to the back to create something from which to hang the frame. You can skip this if you just want to lean the frame against a mirror or a shelf.

6) When the frame is dry, tape your art to the back and enjoy.

This is a great project for kids' rooms!

32 grandma's lace doily pillow

YOU NEED:

- 2 lace doilies,
- ½ yard of matching fabric,
- pillow stuffing,
- sewing machine,
- matching thread,
- scissors,
- needle for hand sewing

Since you can't simply sew two doilies together and fill them with stuffing (they would leak), you have to make a little pillow for the inside first.

1) Measure how much of the edge of the doily that you want hanging over the pillow edge. Subtract twice that amount from the diameter of the doily to figure out how large a pillow you'll need. For example, I wanted to leave a 1½-inch doily border all the way around the pil-

low. The doily's diameter was 16 inches. Subtracting 3 inches from that meant I needed to make a pillow that was 13 inches in diameter.

2) On your fabric, draw 2 circles with the diameter you calculated above. Cut them out and stitch them together on your sewing machine with a ½-inch seam allowance, leaving a small hole to fill your pillow.

3) Stuff your pillow. Hand-stitch the hole closed.

4) Pin your doilies around the pillow and hand-stitch the doilies together with a needle and thread. Simple, beautiful, and elegant!

Several of these on a sofa or a bed will add a wonderfully inviting, warm antique feeling.

33 homemade bathroom *soaps*

YOU NEED:
- **soft glycerin soap,**
- **a Pyrex measuring cup,**
- **microwave,**
- **spray-on cooking oil,**
- **molds (they could be soap or chocolate molds or even a muffin tin)**

Glycerin soaps that are very soft work the best. I used Pears Oil-Clear soap in green.

1) Chop the soap with a sharp knife into ½" x ½" chunks.
2) Melt the soap in the microwave, making sure to check on the progress every 15 seconds. If you leave it in too long, it can get bubbly and start to foam. (Think of a washing machine with too much soap in it!) Keep an eye on it through the microwave door.
3) Spray your mold with cooking spray for easy soap removal. Once the soap is melted, pour it into the molds and let it dry. Leave them alone for at least an hour.
4) Pop them out and wrap in cellophane to give as gifts, or pile them in a soap dish next to your sink.

Tip: Try melting soaps of different colors together!

34 superchic office clip frames

YOU NEED:

- 4 office clips per frame,
- 2 pieces of glass from the same size frame (e.g., glass from two 5" x 7" frames),
- sanding sponge,
- doublestick tape,
- thin wire

1) Make sure that the edges of your glass are not sharp. If they are sharp, sand them a bit with the sanding sponge.

2) Place your art between the pieces of glass (use double-stick tape on the back to help it stay in place if you need to). Add the clips to each side. Use more if you want.

3) To hang, tie some thin wire between the clips in the back.

Tip: I used a graphic copy of the alphabet for this project. Black-and-white photos look great, too.

35 picture clock

YOU NEED:

- favorite photo,
- clock you can easily take apart,
- scissors,
- glue stick,
- pencil,
- sharp craft knife,
- paper,
- glitter glue (optional)

1) Carefully take apart the clock and remove the hands taking note of their order. When replacing the clock hands, it is usually the hour hand first, followed by the minute hand and the second hand, but check before you take them off. Don't bend them!

2) Trace the face of the clock on paper. Enlarge your photo on a color photocopier until it is large enough to fit on the face of the clock. Make sure the image you are using is a bit to the right so you don't cut a hole in their forehead!

3) Using your pattern, cut out the face of the clock from the photocopy. Gently lay the photocopy onto the face of the clock and lightly pencil in where to put your hole for the center. Make sure that you are placing the photocopy in an upright position so you will still be able to tell time. Remove the photocopy and cut out the center hole with a craft knife.

5) Apply the glue stick around the edges of the back of your photocopy and smooth it down onto the clock face. If you made your circle too big, run your craft knife around the edge to remove the excess.

6) Carefully replace the hands of the clock, making sure not to press down too hard. Replace the protective plastic face of the clock.

Add a bit of glitter glue to sparkle it up!

36 gift bag frame

YOU NEED:

- **one gift bag at least 14" x 16",**
- **cardboard,**
- **sharp craft knife,**
- **Elmer's glue,**
- **glass from a 4" x 6" picture frame,**
- **scissors,**
- **tape,**
- **Plumber's Goop Glue,**
- **ribbon,**
- **hot glue gun and glue sticks**

1) Make 2 patterns on a piece of paper: one that is 5½" x 7½" and another that is 4½" x 6½".

2) Cut a 3" x 5" square out of the center of the 5½" x 7½" pattern. Then trace this frame onto a piece of cardboard and cut it out.

3) Trace the 4½" x 6½" inch shape on cardboard and cut it out. This will cover the frame's back.

4) Cut out a 6½" x 8½" piece from your bag.

5) Spread Elmer's glue on the frame with the hole in it, and lay it glue side down in the center of the back of the party bag piece, leaving a ½-inch edge all the way around the frame. Make sure you are gluing it to the back of the party bag!

6) With a sharp knife, cut an X in the center of the frame. You now have 4 triangles in the center of the frame. Evenly spread some Elmer's glue on them and fold

them over. You will have to trim them down a bit. Now spread some more Elmer's glue around the edges and fold them over. Let this dry for about a half hour.

7) After your cardboard frame is covered, glue the glass down on the back with the Plumber's Goop Glue. Tape on your photo and cover the back with the second piece of cardboard. To hang, hot-glue on some ribbon and hang it on a nail.

gift bag wastepaper basket

YOU NEED:

- **trash can that matches your décor,**
- **8½ x 11 piece of paper,**
- **gift bag,**
- **color photocopies of the bag on sticker paper,**
- **pencil,**
- **glue,**
- **McCloskey Heirloom Crystal Clear Polyurethane**

For this wastepaper basket, I took an element of the gift bag that I thought would make a neat design when repeated.

1) Cut out any of the patterns you like from the bag. Paste them on an 8½" x 11" piece of paper.

2) Take this paper to a copy shop and have them make color copies on sticker paper. The number of copies you need will depend on the amount of pattern you can fit on the page and the size of your trash can. I was able to get 6 squares on a piece of sticker paper, and I needed 3 copies for this project.

3) Cut out your designs, and play with their arrangement on the trash can. When you're happy with how it looks, lightly pencil in their placement. Then peel off the stickers' backings, and apply them to your trash can.

4) After you have applied your design, carefully brush on the water-based polyurethane. Once it's dry, you will be able to wipe it clean with a damp cloth.

38 CD case picture boxes

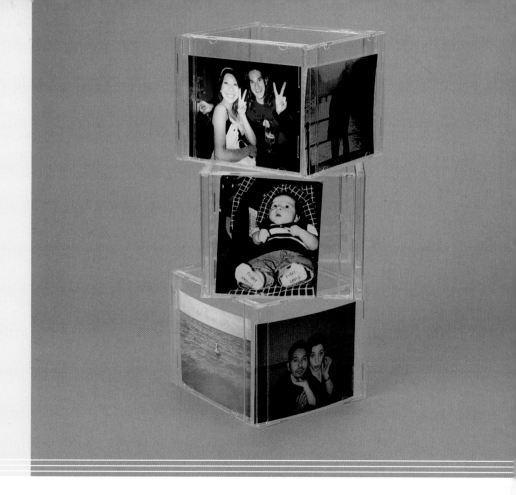

YOU NEED:

- **Plumber's Goop Glue,**
- **4 CD cases per picture box,**
- **sandpaper**

I have been making this project for years because it is so easy, and empty CD cases are just plain fun to make projects with!

1) Carefully snap out and discard the black plastic centers from 4 CD cases. This will leave you with a clear CD case that has a slot on the front side. Sand the side edges with a bit of sandpaper so the glue can adhere better. Glue the cases together on the sides, making sure to leave the slot openings on the outside of the boxes. This will allow you to slide photos in and out easily.

2) Use some cellophane tape to keep them in a perfect square when you are gluing them, and let them dry for at least an hour.

3) You may have to cut your pictures a bit, or you can photocopy them and make them into different sizes to fit the CD cases.

4) The best part about these CD-case picture boxes is that they are stackable, and you can change the photos any time you want. Decorate them with stickers and glitter glue, or even ribbon. You can use your creativity to do anything you want to this basic, very modern-looking project.

39 nail candle-stick holders

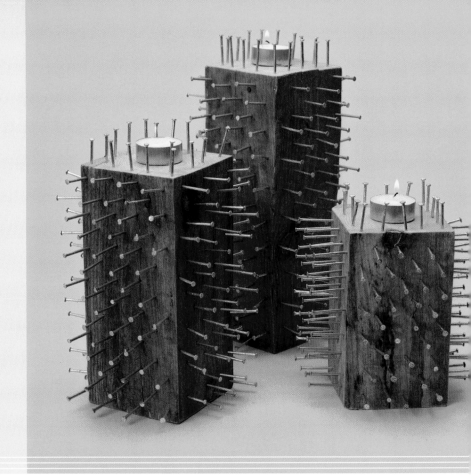

YOU NEED:

- 4" x 4" post that is 8, 12 or 16 inches tall (or all three if you are making a set),
- two to six hundred 2-inch nails,
- hammer,
- earplugs,
- candle in glass or tea lights,
- protective gloves

These posts look great in sets of three at different heights.

1) Ask the lumberyard to cut a 4" x 4" wood post into the length that you want.

2) Lay your wood on its side on a safe surface, like the sidewalk or the driveway because you can damage your floor otherwise! You could do it on a scrap piece of wood, too. But I'd do it in the basement or outside, because it really makes a lot of noise. Start pounding in your nails. Imagine a polka dot pattern and keep the nails about 1 inch apart. Don't pound them in too deep either, only about one inch. Wear some protective gloves—when I was doing this project, I managed to hit my finger a few times just being my normal clumsy self!

3) When you have completed one side of the post, flip it over and do the next side.

4) When you have completed all sides, make a circle of nails around the top of the candleholder to keep your candle in place.

Tip: Place these holders in your fireplace as an alternative to a fire, or use them as a centerpiece for a dinner party.

"tray chic" lamp

YOU NEED:

- **lamp parts,**
- **6 ice-cube trays,**
- **Plumber's Goop Glue,**
- **sandpaper,**
- **cellophane tape,**
- **2 yards of ribbon,**
- **lightbulb fixture with cord,**
- **newspaper**

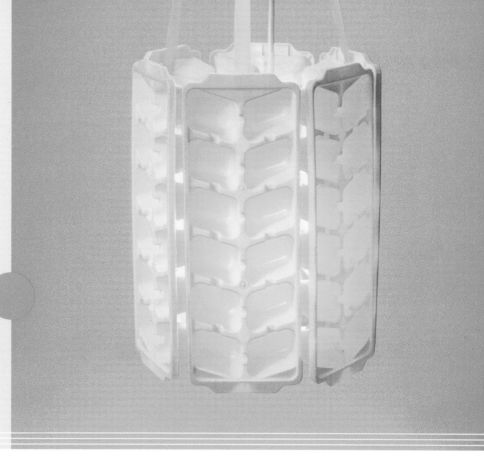

Yippee! I found beautiful yellow ice-cube trays to make this lamp! I usually only see blue trays, and they just don't do it for me.

1) Sand the edges of your ice-cube trays to help the glue adhere.

2) Tape your 6 ice-cube trays together, per the photograph. Lay out newspapers, and carefully add the Plumber's Goop Glue inside the trays to all of the areas where they are touching. Use plenty of glue so you have a very strong lamp.

3) After it dries (give it about 2 hours) add 3 pieces of 14-inch long ribbon to the top center of every other ice tray. Tie the ribbons to the light-fixture cord about 10 inches above the bulb and let it hang. The bulb should be surrounded by the trays.

Now add a little light to your life!

41 fantastic etched dishes

YOU NEED:
- various clear glass dishes,
- etching cream,
- popsicle stick,
- soldering tool with pointy edge or wood burning tool with a pointy edge,
- clear contact paper,
- fine permanent marker,
- protective glasses

Everyone asks me where I got my etched dishes. Now I'm going to let you in on my secret! I use the same technique here that I did with the frosted mirror project (see page 108).

A soldering tool may sound exotic, but you can get them at any dollar store.

1) With the paper still on the back of the plastic, trace your design onto a piece of clear contact paper. Peel and stick the design to your dish.

2) Trace the contact paper design with your hot soldering iron or wood burner. The burner will melt a perfect line around your design, allowing you to peel it away.

3) After you have peeled away the area you wish to etch, carefully spread the etching cream over it with the popsicle stick. Caution: Make sure to follow the instructions on the cream and do not get any of the etching cream on your hands: it is acid and can burn you. Wear pro-tective gloves and be sure to wash your hands frequently while you are working. That said, I made a whole set of dishes without one mishap so don't worry—it's not that dangerous!

4) Leave the cream on for 20 minutes. After 20 minutes, carefully wash it off being careful not to let it touch your skin. Peel off the contact paper, and check out your design.

Tip: You can customize anything with matching designs!

42 box-frame stained-glass lamp

YOU NEED:

- **four 11" x 14" clear plastic box frames,**
- **tissue paper,**
- **small brush,**
- **Elmer's glue,**
- **2 beaded ponytail holders,**
- **scissors,**
- **cellophane tape,**
- **sandpaper,**
- **Plumber's Goop Glue,**
- **small lamp or push light**
- **McCloskey water-based polyurethane varnish**

1) Sand the ends of the clear box frames and glue them together with the Plumber's Goop Glue to make a large box. Goop Glue takes a few minutes to set, so just glue the whole box together at once and add some cellophane tape to keep it in place. Let it dry for about 45 minutes.

2) Cut four beads from the ponytail holders. Sand the beads and glue the sanded edges to the four corners of the bottom of the box.

3) Cut out four hundred 1½-inch squares of tissue in the colors of your choice (I used red and purple).

4) Prepare your Elmer's glue by watering it down a little, just enough to make it more spreadable. (If you make it too watery, just add more glue!) Start at the top and work your way down. Paint a 3-inch square of glue. Lay a tissue square on top of the glue and then paint more glue on top of it. Add another square overlapping the first slightly and paint over that. Make sure to alternate the colors.

5) Continue until the whole box is covered. Let dry for 2 hours.

6) Cover the box with a coat of the water-based polyurethane varnish. Polacrylic works, too. Remember, water-based varnishes are best!

7) Add a small lamp for a light source. You can also use a battery-operated push light.

43 car wash curtains

YOU NEED:

- **3 shower curtains in colors to match your room,**
- **scissors,**
- **shower-curtain rings,**
- **tension rod or curtain rod**

I love car wash curtains because they are whimsical and look like streamers on your window. These are made with three different colors of plastic shower curtains.

1) Cut the shower curtains into 2-inch vertical strips from the bottom up, leaving a 3-inch border intact at the top so you can hang them from simple shower hooks on your curtain rod.

2) Use great color combinations that match your room. Two and three colors look best together!

This would make a great room divider, too!

44 seaweed curtains

YOU NEED:

- **3 shower curtains (2 green, 1 clear),**
- **pinking sheers,**
- **shower curtain rings,**
- **tension or curtain rod**

I designed these curtains for a friend's daughter years ago. She was in love with Ariel the mermaid and wanted an under-the-sea theme for her bedroom.

1) Take three shower curtains (two should be in shades of green and one should be clear) and cut them with pinking sheers. Pinking sheers are scissors that make a zigzag edge when you cut with them. Using this type of scissors will give you the texture and shape you need. Cut strips in the shapes of hands with three fingers, one after the other. When you hang several curtains together you will have something that looks just like seaweed.

2) Hang the curtains from shower curtain rings on a tension rod.

To continue the theme, throw lots of seashells around your room, and add a fish tank or two for shelving. Be sure to go to bed with a snorkel!

drinking straw and faux-flower door beads

YOU NEED:

- **1 box of drinking straws (approximately 300),**
- **scissors,**
- **string,**
- **tension rod,**
- **a 10-inch piece of thin wire,**
- **100 faux flowers**

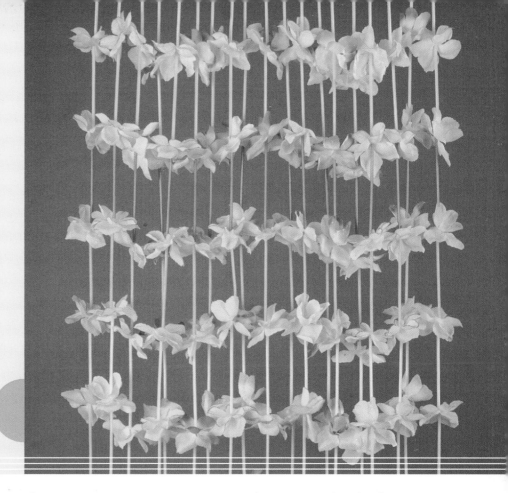

If you don't want to limit yourself to the dollar store, party stores always have a great selection of inexpensive, colorful straws. For this project, I used as many colors as I could find.

1) If your straws are bendable, cut off the part that looks like an accordion—it's hard to work with. And the more straws (and hence the more colors) you use, the better!

2) Take apart your flowers by removing the plastic stems and centers.

3) Create a long needle from a piece of 10-inch wire by simply bending the end into a loop.

4) Thread your needle with about 10 feet of string and start stringing your straws and flowers: Straw, flower, flower, straw, flower, flower, straw, flower, flower, until you get the desired length to cover your door or window. Two petals between each straw look great. Make sure to knot the bottom of

the string around the last flower or all of your work will fall off before you can stop it!

5) Make about 25 strands for an average door. But if you need privacy more than decoration, use more strands. Tie the top of the string to your tension rod.

This project makes a wonderful decoration or favor for a luau!

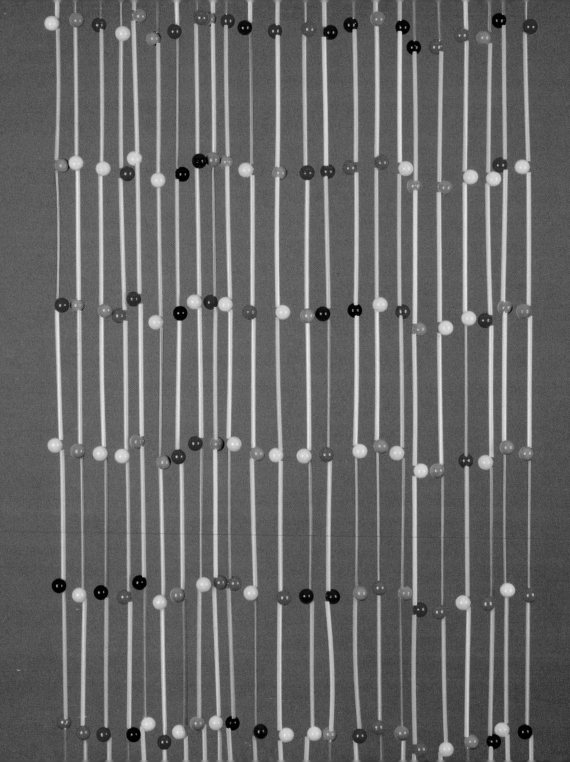

46 drinking straw and ponytail holder door beads

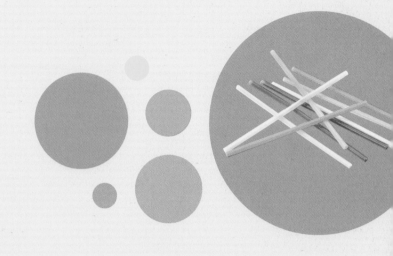

YOU NEED:

- **1 box of drinking straws (approximately 300),**
- **scissors,**
- **string,**
- **tension rod,**
- **a 10-inch piece of thin wire,**
- **about 75 elastic double-bead ponytail holders**

Lately I have been seeing drinking straws in every color under the sun, even black or silver, which would look great with this project! If you don't want to limit yourself to the dollar store, party stores always have a great selection of inexpensive, colorful straws. I used as many colors as I could find.

1) If your straws are bendable, cut off the part that looks like an accordion—it's hard to work with. And the more straws (and hence the more colors) you use, the better!

2) Cut apart your elastic ponytail holders and remove the beads from the elastics. Discard the elastics.

3) Create a long needle from a piece of 10-inch wire by simply bending the end into a loop.

4) Thread your needle with about 10 feet of string and start stringing your straws and beads: Straw, bead, straw, bead, straw, bead, until you get the desired length to cover your door or window. Make sure to knot the bottom string around the last bead, or the beads will fall off at lightning speed. It happened to me several times—and I wasn't happy about it!

5) Make about 25 strands for an average door. If you need privacy more than decoration, use even more strands. Tie the top of the string to the tension rod.

47 wastepaper basket ice bucket

YOU NEED:

- **one really cool wastebasket,**
- **two knobs with screws on the back,**
- **knife**

Isn't it better to have a fantastic ice bucket instead of an ugly cooler to keep your beverages cold when you are eating outside or having a nice dinner? This ice bucket is elegant and easy to make, and you will impress your friends when you tell them how you made it.

1) Select two knobs that screw in from the back—you know, the regular kitchen-drawer knobs that come in tons of different sizes and shapes. I happened upon a dollar store that had a closeout on really great brass knobs.

2) Next, find a trash can with a great shape and color. There are tons out there, so find one that shows your personality or matches your dishes. With a sharp knife, carefully poke holes just big enough for the screw on opposite sides of the basket about 1½ inches down from the rim.

3) Screw on the knobs, fill with ice, and add your favorite bottle of sparkling juice or champagne!

48 cup ball light fixture

YOU NEED:

- 200 3-ounce cups,
- a lightbulb fixture with cord,
- 15 inches of ribbon or chain,
- hot glue gun and glue sticks

1) Hot-glue the cups together at the rims and the bases. Start with 2 cups and keep adding.

2) Keep adding the cups, and you will start to see the ball forming. It takes a while, so be patient! I am always amazed at how long I can spend on a cup ball, but it's always worth it.

3) Leave a hole that is wide enough to allow your lightbulb to be inserted.

4) Glue your chain or ribbon to the cup ball near the opening and attach it to the lightbulb cord about 10 inches up. If you use ribbon, just tie it to the cord; if it's wire, then attach it with a twist tie. Hang it at the desired height from a hook. Use a 25-watt lightbulb.

49 wastepaper basket table

YOU NEED:

- 2 wastebaskets,
- Elmer's Ultimate Glue or Plumber's Goop Glue,
- sandpaper,
- round glass tabletop

Tip: Kmart has decorator tabletops that are 24" in diameter for about $15. This couldn't be any easier if I came to your house and did it for you! To give this project your own personal stamp, try using wastebaskets in two different colors that match your décor—or try making two of the gift bag wastebaskets on page 64 for this project!

1) Sand the bases of the wastebaskets and smear on a generous amount of glue. Lay the glass tabletop on top so it smashes the bases together and helps them bond. Let dry.

2) After the glue dries, lift off the glass top and gently dab 6 dots of the Plumber's Goop Glue on the rim of the top wastebasket. Replace your glass top. This will help it stay in place.

This table is a perfect place for your phone and a small lamp. Two would make wonderful bedside tables!

stunning stained-glass window

YOU NEED:

- **several colors of clear plastic folders,**
- **hot glue gun and glue sticks,**
- **paper,**
- **scissors,**
- **a window or glass frame that you want to hang in a window**

All you need for this project is a lot of imagination and a clean window. The great thing about it is that it is only as permanent as you want it to be. When you are tired of it, just peel it off the glass and make something new!

1) Sketch out the design for your window on a piece of paper. I made flowers, but you can make anything you want: shapes, words, whatever!

2) When you're happy with your design, cut out 2 copies. Tape one copy on the back of your window as a guide for where you want to place your shapes and use the other as a pattern for your plastic pieces.

3) Next, tape your pattern to the plastic folders, trace around them, and cut out the pieces. With a little bit of moisture (OK, lick the backs of the plastic pieces), they will stick nicely to your glass window. Go around the shape with a line of hot glue so it looks like the lead used in real stained glass. Keep it clean with a little bit of glass cleaner on a paper towel.

There is no end to what you can do with this stained-glass technique. You can decorate your windows for the holidays or take down your bathroom curtains and echo your tile work on the window!

51 flower mirror

YOU NEED:

- faux flowers,
- hot glue gun and glue sticks,
- mirror

Try to use a mirror that is at least 8" x 10" so the flowers don't overwhelm it. You want to be able to see yourself surrounded by beautiful flowers!

1) Lightly sand the frame of your mirror.
2) Remove all of the stems and leaves from the flowers, leaving the flowers intact. With hot glue, attach one flower at a time to the frame. Use plenty of glue. Continue around the frame until you have covered it completely.
3) After your flowers are attached, add leaves around the frame to make it pop.

This makes a great gift, and it's perfect for the entrance of your home.

faux-flower frames

YOU NEED:

- **16 faux flowers,**
- **5x7 frame,**
- **hot glue gun and glue sticks,**
- **sandpaper,**
- **scissors**

If you want to make a bigger frame, just buy more flowers.

1) Lightly sand the frame.
2) Remove all of the stems and leaves from the flowers, leaving the flowers intact. With hot glue, attach one flower at a time to the frame. Use plenty of glue. Continue around the frame until you have covered it completely.
3) After your flowers are attached, add leaves around the frame to make it pop.

I like to use simple, colorful photos in this frame because the flowers tend to overwhelm the image. Pick something wonderful, such as a Hindu God or a close-up of someone's face.

53 tissue paper découpage key and change tray

YOU NEED:

- one tray (preferably white),
- tissue paper in three colors
  (I used pink, orange and green),
- Elmer's glue,
- cutouts of flowers,
- scissors,
- small brush,
- McCloskey water-based
  polyurethane varnish

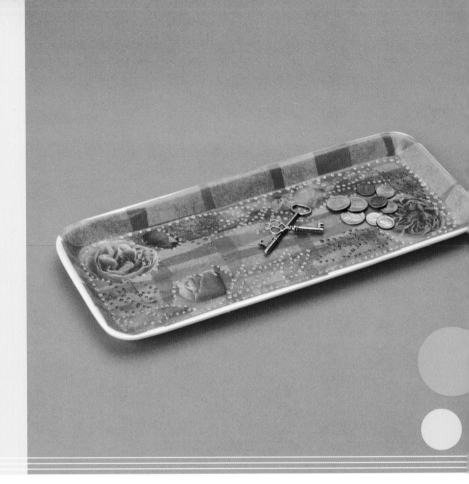

1) Pick a tray with a great shape, preferably white, to make the color of the tissue pop. But if your tray has a small print on it, you can use cutouts of flowers as I did here.

2) Cut about sixty 1½-inch squares of tissue in the colors of your choice (I used orange and pink).

3) Prepare your glue by watering it down a little, just enough to make it more spreadable. (If you make it too watery, just add more glue!)

Paint a 3-inch square of glue wherever you are starting. Add a square of tissue and paint over it again with the glue. Add another square in a different color overlapping it slightly and paint over that. Continue the process until the whole tray is finished. Make sure to alternate the colors. Let it dry for about an hour and a half.

4) Cut out images of flowers from a magazine, then cut out leaf shapes from your remaining tissue color (I used green). Apply these over your first two layers (in my case, pink and orange).

5) Once everything is dry (give it 2 hours to be safe), cover the tray in the water-based polyurethane varnish. Polacrylic works, too. There are several brands at Home Depot that will work for this project, but water-based varnishes are always the best!

flower magnets

YOU NEED:

- inexpensive plastic magnets,
- faux flowers and leaves,
- gems in different sizes,
- hot glue gun and glue sticks

Why not turn your fridge or metal message board into a beautiful bouquet? For this project, look for cheap plastic magnets that have black magnets on the back that you can separate from the decorative plastic.

1) Remove the stems and plastic centers from a few faux flowers.

2) Hot-glue the petals together. You might want to add a leaf or two on the sides like I did, but it's totally up to you!

3) In the center of the top petals, glue a gem. I like to mix and match the colors so it's more exciting to look at.

4) Break apart the magnets from the plastic. Hot-glue the magnets onto the backs of the flowers. Let them dry for a half hour.

Watch your notes and photos bloom on your fridge!

55 rock on rag rug

YOU NEED:
- **4 rag rugs of the same size,**
- **hot glue gun and glue sticks or sewing machine,**
- **ribbon**

Every time I see a rug at the dollar store I wish it was bigger. So I thought, why not sew or glue them together to make a bigger rug? So I did!

1) Line up the rugs end to end and side to side, as in the picture, and hot-glue them together a few inches at a time. Use lots of glue and apply pressure with the palm of your hand to create a good bond. I find that hot glue works wonderfully on fabric because it seeps into the fibers and really sticks together. If you prefer, you could sew these rugs together. It's up to you!

2) After the glue dries, trim the edges of the rug with 1-inch-wide polyester ribbon. You can either glue on the ribbon using hot glue or you can zigzag stitch it with your sewing machine.

$$: This amazing area rug cost less than $5!

sequined candles with charisma

YOU NEED:

- candles,
- 2 packages of ball-head pins,
- sequins in different colors

This project is fun, fast and beautiful. It reminds me of Mexican culture and art, which I love. Find big candles in different bright colors to make this project even more exciting.

1) Take a sequin and attach it to the candle with a contrasting pin. I used the largest sequins I could find, but small sequins would work too. Ball-head pins come in tons of colors, and because they don't have tiny heads like regular straight pins, they are easy to push into the wax without hurting your fingers. Keep adding sequins until the whole candle is covered. Don't worry about a pattern. The more random your colors are, the better the candle will look.

These candles look great in clusters of 2 and 3!

Caution: Remember to always place candles on a glass base or in a large glass container and never leave them burning unattended!

57 candle container chic

YOU NEED:

- **different size drinking glasses or other glass containers,**
- **large candles in glass containers,**
- **newspaper,**
- **scissors,**
- **popsicle sticks,**
- **metal washers,**
- **stove top or microwave**

1) Lay down some newspaper where you are going to work because this project can get messy.

2) There are two different ways to melt down the candles: microwave or stove top. I prefer the latter. Place several of the tall glass candles in a pan half full of water on top of the stove. Gently heat on low until the wax is liquid.

3) Remove the wicks and let them dry. Hold them against the containers you plan to fill. With one end on the bottom of the glass, the other end should extend about ½ inch above the rim of the glass you are filling. Trim the wick to this length. The wicks in these tall candles should be long enough to use for two shorter candles.

4) Tie one end of each wick to a metal washer. This will weigh them down. Tie the other end around a popsicle stick and rest the popsicle stick over the rim of the container you are filling so the wick hangs down perfectly in the center of the container.

5) Pour most of the melted wax into the container and let it harden. Sometimes when you pour your own candles, they harden with a dent in the center. If that happens, use the reserved wax to fill the hole.

Tip: Try using 2 or more colors of wax to make a striped candle!

salad bowl side table

YOU NEED:

- **4-8 large salad bowls,**
- **Plumber's Goop Glue or Elmer's Ultimate Glue,**
- **sandpaper,**
- **round glass tabletop**

Tip: Kmart has decorator tabletops that are 24" in diameter for about $15.

Find 6 plastic salad bowls that look great stacked together. You can even use two different colors that match your décor. Just make sure they are the same shape!

1) Sand the bottoms and tops of the salad bowls. Smear a generous amount of glue onto each and stick them together to form your table base.

2) Lay the glass tabletop on top so that it smashes the bowls together and helps them bond. Let dry two hours.

3) After the glue dries, lift off the glass top and gently dab 6 dots of the glue on the rim of the top bowl. Replace your glass top. Let dry for a half hour.

This table is fun and looks wonderful. It makes a perfect snack table for a dorm room.

59 tissue paper trash can

YOU NEED:
- Elmer's glue,
- ½-inch paintbrush,
- tissue paper,
- scissors,
- white plastic trash can,
- McCloskey water-based polyurethane varnish

Here's another project using my favorite technique of tissue paper and Elmer's glue, which can turn any boring item into a centerpiece.

Tip: Any tissue paper project is great to do with a kid brother or sister.

1) Cut about two hundred 1½-inch squares of tissue in the color of your choice (I used turquoise).

2) Prepare your glue by watering it down a little, just enough to make it more spreadable. (If you make it too watery, just add more glue!) Starting at the top rim of the can and working your way down, paint a 3-inch square of glue. Lay a square of tissue on top of the glue and paint over it again with more glue. Add another square overlapping it slightly and paint over that. Continue the process until the entire trash can is finished.

3) Once it is dry (give it 2 hours to be safe) cover the entire can with water-based polyurethane varnish. Polacrylic works, too. There are several brands at The Home Depot that will work for this project. Remember, water-based varnishes are always the best!

With a trash can like this, you will actually enjoy throwing things away!

60 twig place mats

YOU NEED:
- about 45 twigs of the same size,
- two 2-yard pieces of ¼-inch-wide ribbon

I love this project because it brings nature into the home. Plus, I enjoy spending time outdoors in the fall. However, for these mats, I have to confess that I did use willow branches from a section of willow fencing that you can purchase at most gardening stores. It gives you very even twigs. I have made these place mats in the past with more organically shaped sticks and twigs, and they look even better! The look will be wonderful either way.

1) Gather as many twigs as you will need to make a place mat. I used about 45.

2) Fold a piece of 2-yard-long, ¼-inch-wide ribbon in half. At the fold tie it to your first twig at about 2 inches from the end of the twig. Do the same on the other end of the first twig.

3) Place your second twig next to the first and tie a knot around it next to the knots on the first twig. Continue knotting twigs beside each other until you have the size of place mat that you desire.

4) Leave some extra ribbon hanging off of your last twig so that you can tie your silverware to the place mat and roll it up if you are taking it out for a picnic!

61 hindu god lamp shade

YOU NEED:

- Hindu god art,
- small lamp shade,
- hot glue gun and glue sticks,
- 1 yard of trim,
- glitter glue,
- scissors,
- pencil

Tip: You can use any picture you want for this project.

1) Enlarge your image on a color photocopier to 11" x 17".

2) Before you begin, make sure your image will appear properly on your shade by holding the image and the shade to the light.

3) Lay the copied image printed side down on a flat surface to make your lamp shade pattern. You may want to tape it down. Take your shade, and starting at the seam, carefully roll it on the paper while tracing the top of the shade with a pencil until you get to the seam again and then stop.

4) Keeping the top of the shade aligned with the first line, roll it again, this time tracing the bottom of the shade, starting and ending at the seam. Connect the beginning and end of both lines. Cut out the pattern—it should fit around your shade perfectly.

5) With a hot glue gun, tack the paper around the shade on both the top and bottom. If you need to, trim off any excess with a small pair of scissors.

6) Hot-glue small trim on the seam and then around the top and the bottom of the shade. Now let the light shine in!

hindu god candles

YOU NEED:

- large glass candle,
- Hindu God art,
- color photocopies of the art on sticker paper,
- glitter glue

You can do this with any image, but Hindu gods are so beautiful!

1) Take your image to a copy shop and have it enlarged in color onto 8½" x 11" sticker paper.

2) Before you peel off the protective back, wrap the copy around the candle to figure out where to place the sticker. You may have to trim off some of the image to make it fit on the candle properly.

3) Make a mark on the candle where you want your sticker to start. This way, when you start peeling and sticking, you will be in the perfect position. Carefully peel the sticker from one end of your image and stick that edge to the glass. Peel off the rest of the paper slowly while continuing to stick the image to the glass. This sounds more complicated than it really is!

4) After your sticker is on the glass, pick out several different colors of glitter glue that complement your image. I love gold and red, but take a clue from the image. Recently I have seen packages of glitter glue with up to 15 colors in dollar stores! It's a glitter-glue free-for-all!

5) Make sure to apply only a small amount of glue so it doesn't drip. You can always add more later. Let dry.

Light your candle and enjoy the glow of these wonderful images!

63 lovely leafy mirror

YOU NEED:

- mirror,
- faux flowers with tons of leaves,
- hot glue gun and glue sticks,
- sandpaper,
- scissors

You can use this technique on a picture frame, too!

1) Sand your mirror frame.

2) Next, remove all of the leaves from the flowers, leaving the flower intact so you can use them for other projects (see pages 44, 46, 75, 86, 87, 89, and 141).

3) With hot glue, attach one leaf at a time to the mirror frame. Make some of them poke up in to different directions. Use plenty of glue. Continue around the frame until you have it completely covered.

4) After your leaves are attached, remove any strands of glue that might be left.

64 thumbtack tabletop

YOU NEED:

- **2 boxes of silver or gold thumbtacks (about 300),**
- **a wooden tabletop,**
- **small hammer,**
- **needle-nosed pliers,**
- **pencil,**
- **paper**

$$: I used a $6.99 decorator table from Kmart for this project, but you can spruce up any tabletop or dresser with this tacky technique!

1) With a pencil, sketch your design on a piece of paper the size of the area that you are covering. When you're happy with it, copy it onto the area you will be covering.

2) Hold each tack with a pair of needle-nosed pliers and tap it into the tabletop lightly. (The needle-nosed pliers save your fingers from getting hit with a hammer.) Once each tack is in place, remove the pliers and lightly hammer it into the table. Keep on keepin' on until you are finished with your design. Make sure you don't keep the neighbors up with your hammering!

Tip: If the head of the tack breaks off while you are making your design, remove it with the needle-nosed pliers or just tap in a tack right next to the one that broke.

65 string art tabletop

YOU NEED:
- 1 decorator table,
- 1 glass tabletop,
- pencil,
- 2 boxes of silver or gold thumb-tacks (about 300),
- small hammer,
- 2 colors of yarn (about 1 skein total),
- ruler or tape measure,
- needle-nosed pliers

I used to play with a spirograph when I was little, and this string art technique is like a spirograph drawing come to life. I used a decorator table for this technique, but you can spruce up any tabletop with string art!

1) First, using a tape measure or ruler, mark the placement of a line of thumbtacks 1 inch apart all around the edge of the table you are covering. Number each spot, starting at 1.

2) Holding each tack with a pair of needle-nosed pliers, tap it into the tabletop lightly. (The needle-nosed pliers save your fingers from getting hit with a hammer.) Once each tack is in place, remove the pliers and lightly hammer it into the table, but not all the way. Continue until you have filled all of the numbered spots with tacks.

3) Now it's time to string. Tie a knot around the tack labeled number 1,

and then loop it around the number 30 tack. Come back around to the number 2 tack and then loop it around the number 31 tack. Are you getting it now? Keep looping, 3 to 32, 4 to 33, 5 to 34, 6 to 35 until you have gone all around the table. When you finish, tie another knot on the last tack and you are done. All of the tacks are now connected.

4) For this table I added a second string design in the center with the same technique. You can do this by hammering in another set of tacks nearer to the center of the table and tying another string to these. Be careful to keep the second string above the first pattern so the yarn doesn't get tangled up.

5) When you're done, tap the tacks all the way down into the table to keep everything in place. It's probably best to finish by placing a glass top over the string art to protect your design and to give you a level area on which to place your items.

Tip: If the head of the tack breaks off while you are making your design, remove it with the needle-nosed pliers or just tap in a tack right next to the one that broke.

66 frosted mirror or window

YOU NEED:

- **soldering gun (or wood-burnishing tool) with pointy tip,**
- **mirror,**
- **contact paper,**
- **permanent marker,**
- **printout of letters or image that you are putting on the mirror**

Did you know that you can frost anything with contact paper? It's a great technique that will last forever—as long as you don't peel it off! I used it on my little bathroom window so I could still have light and privacy.

1) Cut your contact paper to the size of the area you are frosting. Lightly trace your pattern onto the contact paper. Contact paper is translucent even with the back still adhered so you can trace anything just by placing the contact paper over it. Or try something freehand! I printed out letters out from my computer to make my name. Circles and stars are great, too.

2) Carefully peel it and stick it to your window or mirror.

3) Take your hot burnishing tool and trace around the parts of the design you wish to peel away. The burnishing tool melts the plastic into a perfect line, making it easy to peel off.

The burnishing tool gets very, very hot, so use caution! As long as you are careful, you can make any design you want.

Tip: If you mess up, you can always peel away the contact paper and start over again.

twine desk set

YOU NEED:

- **2 different colors of twine,**
- **various jars,**
- **cans and boxes,**
- **Elmer's glue,**
- **scissors,**
- **hot glue gun and glue sticks**

There is a wonderful array of twines and strings in the dollar store, and I often purchase them not knowing quite what to do with them other than bundle my recycling! After a while, I came up with the idea of alternating different shades of twine around things to create wonderful crafty stripes, as I did here with this desk set.

1) Hot-glue one end of your twine down to start. Smear Elmer's glue around the area that you are covering so it doesn't slip. Don't worry about overdoing it: the glue will dry clear and you won't be able to see it if it seeps through a bit. Wrap the twine around the area until you have covered 1 inch. Then cut the twine and dot some hot glue on the end to secure it.

2) Start your next shade of twine by dotting some hot glue and wrapping the next inch. Keep alternating adding the stripes and the Elmer's glue until you have covered the entire container.

3) Do this with several containers to create a wonderful desk set for your pencils, pens and office products.

Try this technique with yarn for a different and more colorful look.

68 fabric-covered writing journal and pen

YOU NEED:

- **blank book with hard cover,**
- **pen,**
- **fabric (such as Ultra Suede),**
- **matching ribbon or trim,**
- **hot glue gun and glue sticks,**
- **scissors,**
- **some feathers from a feather duster**

1) Measure your book front to back and top to bottom to make your pattern. Don't forget to add the spine width and add ¾ inch all the way around (top, bottom, and sides) to cover the edges. For example, if you had a book that was 5 inches wide and 8 inches high with a 1-inch spine, your pattern would be 12½ inches across (5" + 5" + 1" + ¾" + ¾") and 9½ inches high (8" + ¾" + ¾").

2) Cut your pattern out of your fabric.

3) Starting with the front cover, position your fabric over the book and glue the top ¾-inch flap over the top edge of the book. It's just like wrapping a present. You will have to clip away the little square of fabric that is over the top of the spine.

4) Now glue the bottom flap. Do the same on the back of the book. Now glue the flap on the front right-hand cover and then the back left-hand cover. Add some trim around the top and bottom edges with more hot glue, being neat!

5) For the pen, take some feathers from a feather duster. Add them around the top of the pen. They come in every color, but I like the natural looking ones. Next, cut a piece of fabric to cover the pen and glue it around the feathers.

6) Finish it off with some trim around the top and bottom of the pen.

twine frame crisscross

YOU NEED:

- 2 different shades of twine,
- frame,
- Elmer's glue,
- hot glue gun and glue sticks,
- scissors

I see twine in the dollar store all of the time and wonder what I should do with it. For years I would wrap presents with it to give them a rustic feel, but after

a while I came up with alternating different shades of twine around things to create stripes as I did here with this frame.

1) Remove the glass and backing from your frame. Secure the end of one shade of twine to the back of the frame with a dab of hot glue to keep it in place. Then wrap it around the inside of the frame.

2) Do about 5 rows of twine across the top, bottom, and sides of your frame, leaving enough space to add your next color. Repeat the process with the other color of twine. Secure in the back with an extra dot of hot glue to make it sturdier.

I framed a postcard I picked up in Italy. You might also try a sepia-toned photo to pick up the natural colors of the twine.

yarn frame crisscross

YOU NEED:

- 3 different colors of yarn,
- hot glue gun and glue sticks,
- Elmer's glue,
- frame,
- scissors

This project was inspired by Mexican tapestries.

1) Remove the glass and backing from your frame. Secure the end of the blue yarn to the back of the frame with a dab of hot glue to keep it in place. Then wrap it around the inside of the frame. I did about 5 rows across the top, bottom, and sides.

2) Take your orange yarn and wrap around the frame next to the blue using the same process. This will create the center stripe, so you might want to make fewer rows than you did with the blue. Again, secure the back with an extra dot of hot glue to make it even more sturdy.

3) Take your purple yarn and wrap around the frame next to the orange on the outer edge of the frame in the same way. This should take up the rest of the space on the frame, leaving you with 3 stripes covering the frame. Remember to secure the yarn to the back of the frame with an extra dot of hot glue.

Tip: If you like to paint, try the fun technique I used to make this watercolor. Drip different shades of paint onto a painted background (mine was yellow). Then sprinkle salt on it while it's wet to give it a splattered texture.

71 scrubber doormat

YOU NEED:

- hot glue gun and glue sticks,
- scissors,
- a 20" x 30" piece of denim or heavy-duty fabric,
- twenty-five 4" x 6" scrubbing pads in different colors,
- newspaper

Hallelujah! They are finally making dish scrubbers in colors other than green! They now have pink, hot pink, orange, blue, yellow, you name it! I made this doormat by gluing 25 of them to a piece of heavy-duty denim.

Tip: Use a generous amount of hot glue for this project because it works best on porous materials and fabrics.

1) Lay out your newspaper. Arrange your scrubbers on the denim until you get a combination that you like. If you want to get fancy, use just 2 colors to make a checkerboard. I did rows of 5 sponges across and 5 sponges down.

2) Start gluing the scrubbers along one edge of the denim using plenty of hot glue. Make sure to get the edges of the sponges so that they don't come up when you step on the mat. Continue gluing down the sponges until you have filled the whole mat. Let dry.

Enjoy a fantastic welcome home!

$$: I found packages of 10 scrubbers for 99 cents and only spent about $3 on this project! If it gets too dirty I can just make another one.

72 seashell mirror

YOU NEED:

- seashells,
- hot glue gun and glue sticks,
- Elmer's glue,
- pearl beads,
- glitter glue,
- 8" x 10" inch mirror with at least a 1-inch-wide frame,
- heavy-duty sandpaper,
- newspaper

My mom loves seashells so this project is for her. I am glad she wasn't around during the photo shoot or she would have put it in her purse.

1) Lay down newspaper. Sand the mirror's frame with sandpaper.

2) Smear on some hot glue and start placing your shells in artful positions. I like to start at the center of each side, then do the corners, then fill in the rest of the sides. Let it dry for about 10 minutes.

3) Once you have your shells hot-glued into place, add a ton of Elmer's glue all the way around for extra security. Don't worry about being messy—just don't get it on the mirror. Tuck it everywhere you can between the shells but don't let the glue dry before going on to step 4!

4) While the glue is still wet, add some pearl beads. I like to take apart the faux-pearl necklaces from the dollar store. Tuck them everywhere you see a little spot that could use one, or go around the center like I did. But don't let the glue dry before going on to step 5!

5) Sprinkle iridescent glitter over everything. Let it dry overnight and wait for the miracle: Elmer's glue dries clear and your mirror will be a masterpiece that Ariel the mermaid would love. My mom will love it, too!

73 glass chip glitter glue frame

YOU NEED:

- glass chips,
- epoxy glue,
- frame with flat edges,
- sandpaper,
- glitter glue in several colors,
- toothpick

Tip: I tried many glues for working with glass chips, and epoxy works the best. You can try hot glue, but check its adherence by trying to remove the glass chip after it's glued. If it comes off easily, use the epoxy. The epoxy takes some time to set, but it's worth it.

1) Find a frame that is flat so that your glass chips won't slide off while you're working. Rounded frames will give you a headache!

2) Mix your epoxy glue on a small paper plate and use a toothpick to apply it to the outer edges of the frame. Carefully place your glass chips around the edges of the frame and let them set for about 5 minutes. You can also dip your glass chip into the glue, but be careful not to get the glue on your fingers.

3) When the glue is set, draw a line of glitter glue around the inside edge of the chips. I used blue because it matched the art I planned to frame. Then trace the outside of the chips in a second color (I used gold).

4) When everything is dry (about 2 hours), insert your art and spruce up that boring wall!

Tip: Several of these together in a cluster will make an amazing statement!

74 pantyhose organizer picture frame

YOU NEED:
- **pantyhose organizer,**
- **small nail**

Pantyhose organizers come in many different colors and make perfect picture frames. They're colorful, easy to hang, quick to change, and you can get a whole party in one frame!

1) Trim your photos to fit the size of the pockets. You can make color photocopies if you don't want to cut the actual photo.
2) Slip the photos into the pockets.
3) Hammer a small nail into the wall and hang your frame!

Tip: I like to keep one on the inside of my closet door so my friends and family greet me every morning. It's just a nice way to start the day.

75 teacup candle

YOU NEED:

- **teacup and saucer,**
- **tall candle in glass,**
- **popsicle stick,**
- **stove top,**
- **metal washer,**
- **newspaper**

1) Lay down some newspaper where you are going to work because this project can get messy.

2) There are two ways to melt down the candles: microwave or stove top. I prefer the latter. Place the candle in a pan half full of water on top of the stove. Gently heat on low until the wax has liquefied.

3) Remove the wick and let it dry. Hold it against the cup you plan to fill. With one end on the bottom of the cup, the other end should extend about ½ inch above the rim. Trim the wick to this length. You should get at least two teacup wicks from the original wick.

4) Tie one end of each wick to a metal washer. This will weigh it down. Tie the other end around a popsicle stick and rest the popsicle stick over the rim of the cup so the wick hangs in the center of the container. Make sure the washer touches the bottom.

5) Wearing oven mitts, fill the teacup with most of the hot wax, being careful not to burn yourself. Sometimes when you pour your own candles they harden with a dent in the center. If that happens, melt the reserved wax to fill the hole.

6) When the wax is dry, remove the popsicle stick and trim the wick.

Tip: These make great shower favors!

tissue paper table

YOU NEED:

- **tissue paper,**
- **Elmer's glue,**
- **small white plastic outdoor table,**
- **small brush,**
- **polacrylic varnish or McCloskey water-based polyurethane**

This tissue paper table is just what you need to brighten an outdoor space! White plastic makes the color of the tissue pop.

1) Cut about two hundred 1½-inch squares of tissue in the color of your choice (I used turquoise and red).

2) Prepare your Elmer's glue by watering it down a little, just enough to make it more spreadable. (If you make it too watery, just add more glue!) Start anywhere on the table and work your way down and around.

3) Paint a 3-inch square of glue on the area in which you are starting. Lay a tissue square on top of the glue and paint more glue on top of it.

4) Add another square overlapping the first slightly and paint over that. Make sure to alternate the colors. Continue the process until the whole table is finished.

5) Once it is dry (give it two hours to be safe) cover it in the water-based polyurethane. Polacrylic works, too. There are several brands at the Home Depot that will work for this project. Remember, water-based varnishes are always the best!

You might love this outdoor table so much that you will have to bring it inside!

77 twine-wrapped lamp base

YOU NEED:

- lamp,
- Elmer's glue,
- hot glue gun and glue sticks,
- 2 rolls of twine

1) Starting under the lightbulb fixture (not on the metal) of the base, secure the end of your twine with a dot of hot glue.

2) Smear Elmer's glue around the area you are covering so that it doesn't slip. Don't worry about overdoing it: the glue will dry clear and you won't be able to see it if it seeps through a bit.

3) Wrap the twine around and around until you have covered the base.

4) If your base has legs like this one, do the legs separately by dotting on some glue and wrapping new pieces of twine down the legs.

Tip: Try this with yarn for a different and more colorful look!

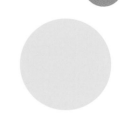

whisk wind chime

YOU NEED:

- 1 whisk,
- wire cutters,
- large glass beads,
- small gauge wire,
- spoons,
- drill,
- ⅛-inch drill bit for metal,
- needle-nosed pliers

1) To make the 5 hanging spoons, cut the loopy bottom part of the whisk (not the handle!) to make 10 individual wires. It will now look like a wire octopus!

2) With the needle-nosed pliers, bend the wires outward making a loop at the end.

3) Drill a hole in the handle of each spoon.

4) Thread the spoons' hole with the thin gauge wire the same way you would thread a needle.

5) Twist the 2 ends of the wire together until it looks like a piece of very thin rope.

6) Thread a bead on the wire and bend the wire around one of the octopus tentacles.

7) Now for the 5 hanging bead pieces: Thread a bead on a piece of wire.

8) Twist the wire until it looks like a piece of very thin wire rope.

9) In the center of the twisted wire, bend a little loop so that you can add another bead and it won't slip down to the bottom next to the other bead.

10) Now bend the end of your beaded pieces over the existing octopus tentacles.

I alternated beaded wire and spoon on my wind chime. You can do it any way you want!

79 lacy cabinet door

YOU NEED:

- screwdriver,
- 2 yards of plastic pantry-liner lace,
- spray paint in a contrasting color,
- tape,
- newspaper

Tip: It may seem like more work to remove the cabinet doors to do the design, but it will actually take you less time to do each door on a table and then reinstall them. I promise!

1) Remove your cabinet door by unscrewing the hinges with a screwdriver.

2) Lay your cabinet door on some newspaper outside (or if you can't go outside, use plenty of ventilation in your work area).

3) Tape your lace onto the outside of the door making sure that the design you want is in the center.

4) Wearing a protective mask so that you don't breathe in the fumes, lightly spray paint over the lace.

5) Lift the corner to see if you have the coverage you want. If not, keep spraying.

6) Let it dry for 1 hour, and then remove the lace.

7) Put your beautiful cabinet door right back up!

(80) spoon cabinet handles

YOU NEED:

- drill,
- ⅛-inch drill bit for metal,
- pliers,
- thin and bendable spoon,
- two ½-inch screws

1) Drill a hole at the top and bottom of your spoon.
2) Carefully bend the spoon into a handle shape.
3) Mark the placement on your cabinet door.
4) Drill in the screws to keep it in place.

Tip: Check out how it looks with the Lacy Cabinet Door. This is also great for dresser drawers!

81 lacy table and chair

YOU NEED:

- **2 yards plastic pantry-liner lace,**
- **gold spray paint,**
- **tape,**
- **dark green plastic outdoor chair and table**

1) Do this outside (or if you can't, use plenty of ventilation in your work area) and wear a protective mask so you don't breathe in the fumes!
2) Tape your lace on your chair or table making sure to center the design.
3) Lightly spray paint over the lace.
4) Lift the corner to see if you have the coverage you want. If not, keep spraying.
5) Let the paint dry for about 5 minutes and then remove the lace. Then let it dry for another 30 minutes.

Sit down and relax in style!

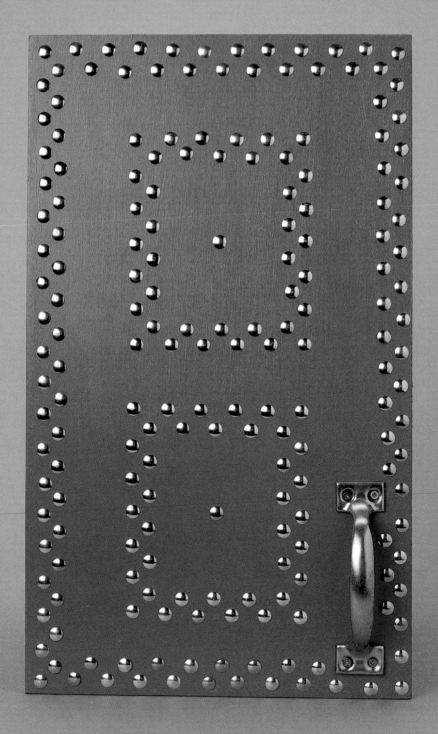

thumbtack cabinet door design

YOU NEED:

- **2 boxes of gold thumbtacks per door (about 200),**
- **cabinet door,**
- **ruler,**
- **small hammer,**
- **needle-nosed pliers,**
- **paper,**
- **pencil**

Tip: It may seem like more work to remove the cabinet doors to do the design, but it will actually take you less time to do each door on a table and then reinstall them. I promise!

1) Remove the cabinet doors and lay them on a work table.

2) With a pencil, sketch your design on a piece of paper the size of the area that you are covering. When you're happy with it, copy it onto the door. Or you can pin the paper over the cabinet door and gently poke the pencil through the paper, dotting the door.

3) Hold each tack with a pair of needle-nosed pliers and lightly tap it into the tabletop. (The needle-nosed pliers save your fingers from getting hit with a hammer.) Once each tack is in place, remove the pliers and lightly hammer the tacks into the table. Make sure you don't keep up the neighbors when you are hammering!

Tip: If the head of the tack breaks off while you are making your design, remove it with the needle-nosed pliers or just tap in a tack right next to the one that broke.

Reinstall your fancy new doors and enjoy!

83) tissue paper-covered jar lamps

YOU NEED:

- tissue paper,
- Elmer's glue,
- clear plastic jar with lid,
- small brush,
- polacrylic varnish or McCloskey water-based polyurethane,
- drill with ¼ inch drill bit,
- lightbulb fixture with cord,
- hook

This is a terrific outdoor lamp.

1) Cut about two hundred 1½-inch squares of tissue in the colors of your choice (I used turquoise and navy).

2) Prepare your glue by watering it down a little, just enough to make it more spreadable. (If you make it too watery, just add more glue!) You can start anywhere on the jar and work your way around. Paint a 3-inch square of glue on the area in which you are starting. Add a square of tissue and paint over it again with the glue. Add another square in a different color overlapping it slightly and paint over that. Continue the process until the whole jar is finished. Make sure to alternate the colors. Let it dry for 2 hours.

3) Once it is dry (give it 2 hours to be safe), cover it in the water-based polyurethane varnish. Polacrylic works too.

4) While it's drying, drill a hole in the center of the lid. Be careful and drill slowly to avoid breaking the plastic!

5) Push your electrical cord through the hole and wire your light socket (it should come with instructions).

6) Add a low-watt light bulb (25 to 40 watts).

7) Screw on the lid and hang from a hook.

Bask in the glow!

84 tissue paper lamp shade

YOU NEED:

- tissue paper in 3 colors,
- pinking sheers,
- Elmer's glue,
- paper lamp shade,
- small brush,
- Polacrylic varnish or McCloskey water-based polyurethane

This lamp shade looks like a million bucks!

1) Cut about two hundred 2½" x 2" leaf shapes out of the 3 colors of tissue paper (I used fall colors).

2) Prepare your glue by watering it down a little, just enough to make it more spreadable. (If you make it too watery, just add more glue!) You can start anywhere on the shade and work your way around.

Paint a 3-inch square of glue on the area where you are starting. Add a leaf and paint over it again with the glue. Add another leaf overlapping the first slightly and paint over that, making sure to put a darker color next to a lighter color in a falling-leaf pattern. Continue the process until the whole shade is finished. Let it dry for 2 hours.

3) Once it is dry, cover it in the water-based polyurethane varnish. Polacrylic works, too. This will give it a nice protective sheen and make it easy to dust.

hanging votive holders

YOU NEED:

- tapered drinking glass (wider on the top than the bottom),
- metal plumber strapping with holes the size of a hole punch hole every inch,
- sheet metal cutters,
- 2 yards of small gauge wire chain,
- wire cutters,
- small ceiling hook,
- votive candles

1) Cut three 12-inch pieces off of your 2-yard piece of chain.

2) Cut a small piece out of the last link on each 12-inch chain to make hooks.

3) Measure the circumference of the top of your glass and add an inch. This will be the length of plumber strapping you'll need for the band around the top of the drinking glass (you want it to overlap which is why you add an inch). Plumber's strapping is a ¾-inch-wide metal with holes used for securing pipes. It comes in a roll and is easy to cut with heavy-duty scissors or tin snips. It's also bendable and easily secured to the glass as long as the glass tapers from the top to the bottom.

4) Wrap the plumber strapping around the glass, overlapping the ends and hooking the open link on the end of your 12-inch-piece of chain through the overlapped holes.

5) Attach the other 2 pieces of chain equally around the strapping.

6) Hook all three 12-inch pieces of chain to the remaining 1 yard piece of chain.

7) Add a votive candle and hang from a ceiling hook.

Beautiful for a party!

86 terrific topiary lamp

YOU NEED:

- **lamp with a thin base,**
- **lamp shade,**
- **hot glue gun and glue sticks,**
- **3 yards of brown ribbon,**
- **tons of faux leaves**

1) To make your tree trunk, begin at the top of the lamp base under the bulb hardware. Dab a bit of hot glue at the top (under the metal fixture) and attach one end of your ribbon. Wrap it around and around the base all the way down.

2) When you get to the base, either keep wrapping or make stripes. My lamp base was flat so I had to glue strips across it. The key is to find a way to cover the entire base with brown ribbon!

3) Hot-glue a few leaves to the base make it look more treelike.

4) For the shade, start at the base of the shade and glue the leaves right next to one another, overlapping them a bit. When you complete the first row, start the row above it overlapping the row below it by about ¼ inch.

5) When you get to the top, fold the leaves over the edge so they cover the top edge of the shade to finish the look.

It's kind of easy being green!

⑧⑦ faux rag rug cabinet door

YOU NEED:

- cabinet doors to decorate,
- rag rug with colors that you like,
- color photocopies of the rug on sticker paper,
- simple door handle,
- Polacrylic varnish or McCloskey water-based polyurethane

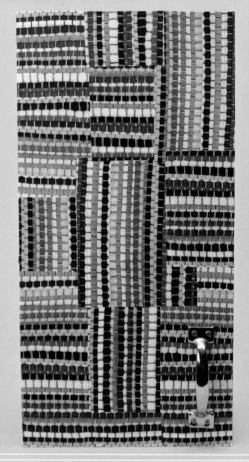

$$: I found the handles used here in pairs for 99 cents!

1) Take your rug to a copy shop and have it color copied onto sticker paper. Measure your doors before you go to see how much sticker paper you will need (it usually comes in 8½" by 11" sheets).

2) Clean and dry your cabinet door. Remove the handles. It will make the process go more quickly and will look neater!

4) Decide how you want to place your stickers, then peel and stick them to the doors.

5) Paint over the doors with the water-based polyurethane to give it a protective finish.

6) Replace your old handles or add some new ones.

Tip: Make a big rag rug to complete the look! See page 90.

bouquet breakfast tray

YOU NEED:

- **12" x 24" x ½" piece of birch plywood,**
- **2 handles,**
- **1 document frame,**
- **Plumber's Goop Glue,**
- **latex high-gloss paint,**
- **drill with screw bit,**
- **faux flowers,**
- **hot glue gun and glue sticks**

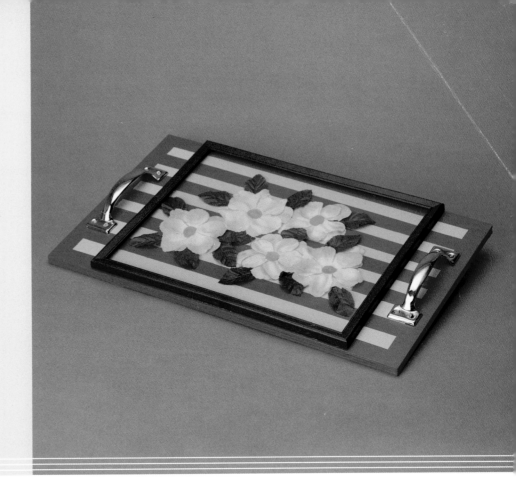

What I really like about this tray is that it's a beautiful piece of art when it's not in use. It looks great just leaning against the wall on a shelf.

1) Paint your board any way you want. I painted mine with dark pink first, let it dry, then blocked off stripes with masking tape, and filled in every other one with a lighter pink. Let it dry for 45 minutes.

2) Take apart your faux flowers and hot-glue them to the center of the painted board.

3) Add some leaves around the edges.

4) Remove the cardboard from the back of the document frame and add a line of hot glue all around the inside of the frame to secure the glass. Let it dry for 15 minutes.

5) Add the Plumber's Goop Glue to the back of the frame and glue the frame down over the flowers. Let it dry for about 20 minutes.

6) Place your handles on the edge of the tray and, using a screwdriver, screw them on. The key here is to find handles that screw in from the top instead of from underneath.

Serve up some breakfast in bed!

89 drinking glass vases

YOU NEED:

- **two drinking glasses per vase,**
- **epoxy glue**

Next time you are in the dish section of the dollar store, start putting the glasses bottom to bottom and see what you come up with. The variations are endless, and they make wonderful vases or centerpieces for a wedding! You just have to experiment.

1) Clean and dry glasses thoroughly.
2) Mix epoxy glue on a paper plate.
3) Spread evenly on the bottom of one of the glasses.
4) Carefully place the other glass bottom on top on the glue. Let it set for about 20 minutes.
5) Fill with water and flowers!

bandanna curtains and pillow

YOU NEED:

- **5 yellow and 5 turquoise bandannas,**
- **sewing machine,**
- **matching thread,**
- **pillow stuffing,**
- **curtain rod,**
- **needle and thread,**
- **iron**

There were so many wonderful colors of bandannas in the dollar store, I could hardly decide what looked best together. I finally went with yellow and turquoise because it was bright, fun, and, let's face it, I love color!

1) Iron your bandannas.

2) Pin four of them together in a strip, alternating colors.

3) Stitch them together.

4) Clip any loose threads.

5) Fold the top over 1½ inches and stitch along the fold to make a pocket for your curtain rod.

6) Repeat this process to make the other panel.

7) To make the pillow, pin together the remaining two bandannas and stitch them together using a 2-inch seam allowance, leaving a 4-inch hole in which to fill your pillow. The 2-inch seam allowance will give a wonderful decorative edge to your pillow.

8) Stuff the pillow.

9) Stitch the hole closed.

plastic fantastic container lamps

YOU NEED:

- **2 plastic containers,**
- **small gauge wire,**
- **wire cutters,**
- **drill,**
- **⅛-inch and ¼-inch drill bits,**
- **lightbulb fixture with cord,**
- **pencil,**
- **hook**

You want to look for two plastic containers that look great together. There are so many containers to choose from at the dollar store that I am sure you will find something wonderful!

1) Place the openings of the plastic containers together.

2) With a pencil, mark 3 sets of matching holes on the mouths of both containers. (Eventually you will drill these holes and attach the mouths of the containers together with small gauge wire.)

3) Using an ⅛-inch bit, drill the 6 holes.

4) Drill a ¼-inch hole in the center of the base of one container.

5) Thread your cord through the ¼-inch hole and attach your light socket and bulb.

6) Line up the containers mouth to mouth again and thread the small gauge wire through the matching holes, twisting the wire to keep the mouths together.

7) Hang from a hook and light up your life!

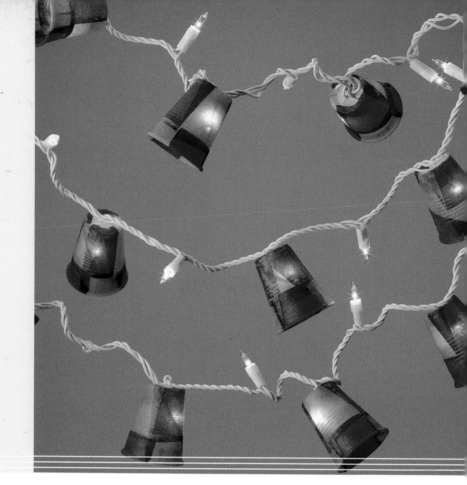

92 party lights

YOU NEED:

- string of Christmas tree lights in white,
- 3-oz. plastic cups,
- tissue paper in 2 colors,
- sharp craft knife,
- Elmer's glue,
- paint brush,
- scissors

1) Cut about two hundred 1" x 1" squares out of 2 colors of tissue paper (I used red and turquoise).

2) Prepare your glue by watering it down a little, just enough to make it more spreadable. (If you make it too watery, just add more glue!) Paint a 3-inch square of glue on a cup. Lay a tissue square on top of the glue and then paint more glue on top of it. Add another square overlapping the first slightly and paint over that. Make sure to alternate the colors and continue the process until the cup is covered. Repeat on the other cups.

3) Once it is dry (give it two hours to be safe), cover it in the water-based polyurethane varnish. Polacrylic works, too. This will give it a nice protective sheen. Let it dry for about 20 minutes.

4) With the craft knife, cut an "X" in the base of a cup and slip it over a light. Christmas lights don't get very hot so this is fine, but as with all lights, don't leave them on when you're not around!

5) Cover the rest of the lights with the other cups and have a party!

93 padded headboard with thumbtack design

YOU NEED:

- 2 yards of batting,
- 2 yards of denim,
- staple gun,
- staples,
- scissors,
- brass thumbtacks,
- needle-nosed pliers,
- marking chalk,
- 4" x 4" x ½" piece of plywood,
- pencil,
- hammer

1) Fold your batting around the wood and staple it on the back.

2) Fold the denim around the padded wood and staple it to the back. You now have what looks like a padded denim square.

3) Sketch your thumbtack design onto a piece of paper.

4) When you're happy with it, copy it onto the padded headboard with a pencil.

5) Holding each tack with the needle-nosed pliers, tap it in to the headboard with the hammer.

6) Continue your design until you are finished.

Remove your old headboard and place this one at the head of your bed!

tin candlestick chandelier

YOU NEED:

- **3 tin candlesticks,**
- **small gauge wire,**
- **wire cutters,**
- **beads on wire,**
- **gold spray paint,**
- **light parts,**
- **lightbulb fixture with cord,**
- **1-inch ribbon,**
- **newspaper**

When I saw these candlesticks, I just knew I could do something wonderful with them. I turned them upside down and wired three of them together to form the base of this chandelier. You may not find the same ones, so be creative!

1) Wire the candlesticks together at the base and at the top, where they meet, to form the chandelier.

2) Lay down some newspaper outside or in a well-ventilated area and, wearing a protective mask, spray paint the whole thing gold.

3) Wrap your beads around the chandelier.

4) Wire the lamp parts together by attaching the light socket to the electrical cord.

5) Tie 3 pieces of ribbon to the top of the chandelier and tie those ribbons to the cord.

6) Hang it by the ribbons from a hook.

Tip: I found the beads used here at a flower supply shop, but you can find this stuff anywhere—try stationery and bead stores for things to add sparkle to your new chandelier!

95 laminated brown paper bag trash can

YOU NEED:

- **2 large brown paper bags of the same size,**
- **clear contact paper,**
- **scissors**

This is nifty!

1) To make a pattern for your contact paper, cut one of the bags apart so that you have a front, a side and a bottom. Since you are covering the inside and the outside of the bag, you will need to cut 2 of each pattern. Trace these pattern pieces on the contact paper.

2) Take the remaining bag and stick the contact paper to the appropriate parts. Position your contact paper on each part of the bag before you peel off the protective back to make sure it's straight. The contact paper should cover the bag completely inside and out. Don't worry if it gets wrinkled because that is what makes it look great!

OK, have I lost my mind? I absolutely love this design and think it is very witty!

96 striped tissue paper candleholders

YOU NEED:

- glass containers in various sizes,
- Elmer's glue,
- ½-inch paint brush,
- tissue paper,
- scissors

1) Cut about thirty ½-inch wide strips out of 2 colors of tissue paper (I used pink and purple). They should be 2 inches longer then the glass you are covering.

2) Prepare your Elmer's Glue by watering it down a little, just enough to make it more spreadable. (If you make it too watery, just add more glue!) Start at the top of the glass and work your way down. Paint a stripe of glue onto the glass container. Add a strip of tissue starting at the mouth of the glass and continuing down to the base. When you get to the base, fold the strip under and glue it to the bottom of the glass and paint over it again with the glue. Add another strip of tissue right next to the first, overlapping it slightly, and paint over that. Continue the process until the container is covered.

3) Cut a circle that is just a bit smaller than the bottom of the container and glue it to the bottom to cover the ends of the strips. Leave the glass on its mouth to dry.

4) Once it is dry (give it 2 hours to be safe) cover it in the water-based polyurethane varnish. Polacrylic works, too. This will give it a nice protective sheen.

Put in a candle and see how beautifully it glows. Or fill it with jewelry or seashells! It's up to you.

97 CD photo headboard calendar

YOU NEED:

- 4 'x 4' piece of birch plywood,
- latex paint in a bright color like hot pink,
- paintbrush,
- sandpaper,
- 43 CD cases with the black plastic centers removed,
- hot glue gun and glue sticks,
- printouts of the days of the week,
- printouts of the numbers 1 through 31,
- pencil,
- newspaper

1) Lay down some newspaper in a well-ventilated area and paint your wood. Let it dry for about 2 hours.

2) Center the top row of 7 CD cases on the top of the painted board. Lightly mark their placement with a pencil.

3) Sand the backs of the cases and glue them on the board so that the slot opening is in the front left hand side of the CD so that you can slip in the letters and numbers of your calendar.

4) Print out your numbers and letters in a very large font or just write them out.

5) Cut them out so that they fit into the CD cases and fill in your calendar.

Make some time!

98 butterfly headboard

YOU NEED:

- 4' x 4' piece of birch plywood,
- jigsaw,
- pencil,
- butterflies,
- 2 colors of green paint,
- small paintbrush,
- large paintbrush,
- drill and screws or Plumber's Goop Glue

You can get these butterflies at any dollar store.

1) Cut your headboard into a leafy shape with the jigsaw. It doesn't have to be just like mine: You can experiment and the butterflies will cover any mistake you might make.

2) With your large brush, paint it green in a well-ventilated area. Let it dry for 2 hours.

3) With your small brush, paint the details around the leaves in the other color of green and let that dry for another hour.

4) Drill a hole into each butterfly and attach each to the headboard with a screw or a nail. If you don't want to use a drill, use Plumber's Goop Glue instead.

Welcome to your secret garden!